TEACHING
YOUR CHILDREN
ABOUT GOD

ALSO BY DAVID J. WOLPE

*The Healer of Shattered Hearts: A
  Jewish View of God*

*In Speech and In Silence: The Jewish
  Quest for God*

TEACHING
YOUR CHILDREN
ABOUT GOD

A Modern Jewish Approach

DAVID J. WOLPE

Henry Holt and Company
New York

Henry Holt and Company, Inc.
Publishers since 1866
115 West 18th Street
New York, New York 10011

Henry Holt® is a registered
trademark of Henry Holt and Company, Inc.

Published in Canada by Fitzhenry & Whiteside Ltd.,
195 Allstate Parkway, Markham, Ontario L3R 4T8.

Library of Congress Cataloging-in-Publication Data
Wolpe, David J.
Teaching your children about God / David J. Wolpe.
p.   cm.
Includes bibliographical references and index.
1. God (Judaism)—Study and teaching.   2. Jewish
religious education of children.   I. Title.
BM610.W65   1993   93-2294
296.3'11—dc20   CIP
ISBN 0-8050-2616-9

Henry Holt books are available for special promotions and
premiums. For details contact: Director, Special Markets.

First Edition—1993

Designed by Katy Riegel

Printed in the United States of America
All first editions are printed on acid-free paper.∞

1   3   5   7   9   10   8   6   4   2

TO EILEEN

Contents

Acknowledgments

The University of Judaism is a wonderful place to teach, and to learn. I'd like to thank the University's president, Dr. Robert Wexler, as well as the faculty and staff, who are a constant source of support.

In my years of teaching children I have had the opportunity of working with some wonderful educators. Two in particular, Dr. Alvin Mars and Mrs. Sara Cohen, taught me a great deal about how to speak with children about life, and about God.

My thanks to Mimi Sells, Sam Mitnick, Marc Platt, Nama Frenkel, Robin Graff, and Dr. Gail Dorph, all of whom helped shepherd this book along in various ways.

My editor, Marian Wood, is possessed of marvelous insight. I am glad to have come once again under her watchful and generous eye.

I am also grateful to thousands of children over the years who have shared with me their ideas, aspirations, and fears. I hope this book is some return on their investment in an adult.

One's own childhood is the first learning ground. I was very lucky to be born into an extraordinary family. Steve, Paul, Valerie, Danny, and my parents were, and are, my perpetual teachers.

Finally, thanks to Eileen, for gifts that transcend expression.

Preface

"We are born believing," wrote Emerson, "a man bears beliefs as a tree bears apples."

Parents who listen to their children's words hear belief. Children do have a natural capacity for faith. But all too often their faith is untended and lost.

Faith is untended because we as teachers and parents do not know how to react to religious questions. We find it hard to talk about God. If our children don't ask, we maintain a grateful silence. If they do ask, we give the briefest of answers and pass on to other subjects. But we know inside that this will not do. Adults pride themselves on being open to all sorts of discussions. We will arm ourselves to answer questions about sexuality, friendship, family—anything. We are ready to delight in children's insights. Yet we are stumped when the subject is the most important subject of all: Where do we come from? What does life mean? Is there a God, or are we alone in this world?

Sometimes we duck the question for the same reason we

don't help with math or history homework—we simply don't know the answer. It is easier to send the child to the local expert—to the clergy or the religious school teacher. Yet we are supposed to be giving direction to the lives of our children. There are many other areas of life where we do not know the answer, but we are willing to talk and to teach. Why should the critical area of spiritual growth be any different?

This book is a result of years of speaking about God to adults and to children. The forums have varied—synagogues, churches, summer camps, and schools—but the questions remain constant. This book contains many of the questions, answers, and stories that I have learned over those years. It is directed to parents, but it can be used by teachers, counselors, youth directors—all who want a sense of how to respond to the questions our children ask. But it is parents, both couples and single parents, who have the primary role in developing a child's intellect and character, parents who have the primary role in shaping their child's soul.

This book deals primarily with responses to the serious religious questions beginning to be asked by children about ages four to fourteen. There are discussions suitable for older children, and answers suggested for younger children as well. But the focus is on the crucial years from post-toddler to adolescent, when the questions come fast and furious.

There are no certain or absolute answers to these questions. There is no religious cookbook for difficult issues. There are, however, responses that seem more helpful and more encouraging than others.

The exercises in the book are designed to help put some

of the ideas into practice. Each chapter begins with a summary, and concludes with questions intended to stimulate further exploration together with your children. The list of commonly asked questions in the appendix is for easy access to the key ideas contained throughout the book. Finally, there are some suggested readings for those who wish to pursue this topic further.

Relevant studies teach us that all children have an image of God. Even those who grow up in a home without religion develop ideas about God and images of God. The question is whether we can guide those images, understand them, and learn from them.

Rabbi Meir taught the following:

When the Israelites came to the mountain of Sinai to receive God's word, the Torah, they discovered that God was not willing to give it without proof that they would cherish this precious gift. So God said to Israel: "Give Me guarantors that you will treasure My Torah." The people of Israel said: "Our ancestors will be our guarantors." God answered: "They are not sufficient. I have found fault with your ancestors. They would need guarantors for themselves!" The Israelites spoke again: "If You will not accept our ancestors, accept our Prophets—they will vouch for us." But God answered: "I have found fault with your prophets as well. They too would need their own guarantors. You may try one more time." The Israelites, newly freed from the slavery of Egypt, looked up to the heavens and said to God: "If You will give us Your Torah, we will offer You our children." And God said: "Since you offer Me your children, I will give you My Torah."

(Song of Songs *Rabbah* 1:4)

And so God's word is entrusted to our children. Our children are entrusted to us.

Finding God Ourselves: Rediscovering Our Spiritual Roots

A man came to his rabbi and said: "Rabbi when I was a child I felt very close to God. Now that I am older, it seems as if God has left me, or perhaps it is I who have left. In either case, I feel far from God. I am not sure what to do." The rabbi answered him, "When you teach a child to walk, at first you stand very close. The child can only take one step, and then you must catch him. But as he grows, you move farther and farther away, so that he can walk to you. God has not abandoned you. Like a good parent, God has moved farther away, but is still close by, waiting for you. Now you must learn to walk to God."

MANY OF US have lost the certainties of our childhood. Yet, now we face the need to teach our own children about God. To help them search for faith we must try to understand some things anew for ourselves.

We want to create a family atmosphere that has sacred moments and a feeling of warmth. We want to encourage our children to question and to search. We want to make sure they learn how important it is both to be good and to feel that they matter.

Religion can help in all these critical areas of growth. Belief in God affects self-esteem, and searching for God together can help draw a family close.

By opening a dialogue with our children, we can develop a faith that is modern and honest, a faith true to tradition and to the search for God.

———

When I was seventeen, the synagogue I attended as a child moved to a new building. I remember writing a poem about visiting the old building after everything had been packed up and everyone had gone. There were seats, but no worshipers. There was an ark to hold the Torah scroll, but it was empty. The sanctuary, which for so long had been sacred, was hollow and sad.

The poem was a metaphor for losing my own faith. I had attended this synagogue since the age of ten. It was the place where I had grown from a child's belief in God to an adolescent's skepticism about all religion. In particular I remember, while I wandered about in the abandoned sanctuary, looking up at the eternal light hanging above the ark. The lamp is supposed to flicker forever, symbolizing God's eternal presence. It was out, and I left.

For many of us, God is absent. We hear about God and we might occasionally invoke God at ceremonies or observances. But God is not part of our days and nights. God is not a living presence.

We may have lost God in childhood, in high school or college. For some, a family tragedy proved that God was unreal or unreliable. For others, adulthood is simply a time to cast off old beliefs and ideas. Perhaps we never really had a sense of God. Perhaps we never cared. Perhaps only now are we being asked.

Often the questions come from our children. Their questions, fears, and wonder at times make us want to reenter the sanctuary. But many of us left that empty sanctuary years ago, and we do not know how to get back in. Both for ourselves and for our children, it is important to reopen the door, blow the dust off the seats, and see if we can't find inside some long overlooked inspirations. Perhaps the lamp hanging above the ark is called an eternal light not because it burns continuously, but because even if it goes out, it can always be rekindled.

WHY IS IT SO HARD TO TALK ABOUT GOD?

We are suddenly embarrassed and uncomfortable when our children ask us about God. It is as if we had an old friend whom we have neglected, and suddenly someone asks us how our friend is, not realizing we have fallen out of touch. We feel guilty. Possibly we are just annoyed at having to deal with something we left behind so long ago. We sidestep the question. Our children are left without an answer and unsatisfied.

Children have very sensitive antennae. They pick up the discomfort of adults no matter how skillfully hidden. In time, children learn that to ask about God does not bring help; their parents do not know how to answer. They will themselves grow up without the vocabulary to talk about God to their own children.

A spiritual education is as important to a full life as an intellectual and emotional education. As much as we need an attitude toward the visible world, we need an attitude toward the ineffable, the world beyond what can be seen. Living well means living with some sensitivity toward all we cannot see, forces in the world that are over and above us, and even within us. What we believe about God greatly affects how we view ourselves, other people, and our world.

In poll after poll, Americans affirm that they believe in God. The percentage of Americans who affirm some type of belief consistently rises above 90 percent. Yet for many of us, life is lived without discussion of God, without learning about our own religious traditions.

An old saying has it that there are three things we should not discuss in polite company: sex, politics, and religion. We certainly don't follow the advice of that proverb when it comes to sex and politics. Together, they make up most of our conversation. The politics of the office as well as of the nation are constantly discussed. Sexuality, especially in the larger context of relationships, is a constant topic of conversation. The third theme alone is missing.

We carefully avoid discussion of religion. That one great subject is untouched. At your next party, try sidling up to someone, drink in hand, and asking, "So what do you think about God, anyway?" You will quickly find yourself alone. Faith does not enter our conversations. Everyone has his or her own ideas about God, we explain; but that is equally true of sex and politics. It is too personal, we say; but surely sex is personal as well. The truth seems to be that most of us are deeply embarrassed about discussing the most important issues of life. This lack impoverishes our conversation, and ultimately our lives as well.

We need to reestablish the rightness of talking about religion with adults. Tearing oneself away from daily tasks and the usual topics is not easy. We need to talk about ultimate issues. We need to open spaces in ourselves that will help to encourage the conversation.

THE FEELING OF HOLINESS

Children learn how to identify feelings as they grow. They identify the warmth they feel inside as "love." The feeling of needing to explode is "anger." If given the chance, they can also learn to call the sense of high connection "sacred." With an idea of God, certain things are not only beautiful, or good, but "holy."

Holiness is a special realm, a short step from the magical imaginations of children. Children listen to fairy tales with a sense that there are great things at stake. Castles and dragons and kingdoms are another way of saying that in this story the issues are terribly important. The characters have momentous decisions to make, and their actions have real consequences. The realm of the sacred is about enchantment that really exists, a feeling of magic one can find by being in the world. With God, with holiness, we feel the importance of our actions. Goodness becomes not only a proper choice, but a cosmic act. We elevate our actions and become players in a great saga.

For all the elements of story and make-believe in religion, sanctity is as real as all the other things children learn to value in their lives. When the biblical character Jacob first leaves home, he has a marvelous dream. In his dream he sees ladders connecting heaven and earth, and angels ascending and descending the ladders. When he wakes up, he exclaims: "Surely God is in this place, and I did not know it (Gen. 28:16)!" Jacob felt the magical touch of sanctity in a place he thought was ordinary. He finds out that the sacred is real, even if he has to first discover it in a dream.

Sometimes children have an experience of the sacred in dreams, or in play, or in prayer. Often they need us to identify what it is they feel. When children have an experience of the sacred, it deepens their souls. They find out, as did Jacob, that there is another part of life they had not suspected.

When we teach our children about God, we are also teaching them how to feel a sense of the sacred. It is a feeling they would otherwise miss. Perhaps without teaching them, we would miss it too.

◆ ◆ ◆

Exercise 1—Looking for Sanctity. Go alone with your child to a sanctuary. You will probably have to get permission to go, because you want to find a time when just the two of you are there. Late in the day is a wonderful time, but it must be when it is still light, so that the natural light (often through stained-glass windows) shines in. Walk around. Feel the quiet and the sense of grandeur. Stand before the ark, under the eternal light, just you and your child. That feeling is sanctity.

———

KNOWING THAT GOD CARES AND UNDERSTANDS

To children, the world is something of a foreign country. It is ruled by adults, who are not wholly understood. Many of the things in this world are closed off to children: they cannot drive cars or eat as they please or buy anything they want or go places alone. No matter how hard adults try to sympathize with them, part of the child will always feel cut off from the adult world. Children's books constantly explore this theme—the child alone in a world where no one fully understands.

Nothing could be more important than to feel that someone always cares and really understands. For a child to believe in God's concern is not an intellectual proposition or a philosophical decision. It is a way of trusting in the goodness of the world. It is a way of asserting that one is not alone. It is to have what is called in Hebrew *bitachon,* "trust," a sense of confidence that runs deep inside because it flows from above.

Bitachon can help give children a sense of security. They are connected to this often strange world. The novelist Joseph Conrad wrote, "Woe to the man whose heart has not learned while young to hope, to love, and to put his trust in life." To have faith is to assert a basic trust in life, sometimes in the face of its unfairness. Such trust is a priceless legacy to a child. And in teaching children trust, we become more trusted, and perhaps more trusting, ourselves.

WRESTLING WITH GOD

For many, our religious education stopped in childhood. In Jewish circles people often abandon any sort of religious training at Bar Mitzvah. As a result, their ideas about religion are those suitable for twelve- and thirteen-year-olds. Not surprisingly, at age twenty or thirty or fifty, such notions seem simple. They are simple. The French artist Jean Cocteau tells the story of his small niece, whose mother came home one day and said, "An angel brought us a baby. Would you like to see your new brother?" The little girl answered, "No—I want to see the angel." A child who answers that way is already beginning to outgrow some of the religious ideas she has been taught.

Religious ideas, like political ideas, need to grow as one matures. Even though we begin by teaching religion to children, its deepest ideas unfold only if we study it as adults.

To make matters worse, many who did have a religious education are filled with resentment when they recall their experiences. Some found that their teachers were uninterested in real teaching; they just wanted to open their students' heads and pour ideas in. Others found that the teachers had no sense of children's needs. One woman in her sixties who was returning to her religious roots said to me: "If I had been taught English the way I was taught Judaism, I would never speak a sentence." She felt cheated. She was right.

The traditional name of the Jewish people is "Israel," which derives from the biblical story of Jacob's wrestling with an angel. "Israel" means a "wrestler with God." We are supposed to wrestle with God, with the idea of God, with the traditions taught in God's name. Those of us who recall a religious education without exchange and excitement know that more wrestling was what we needed.

Faith is about trust, but it is also about struggle. Now that we are teachers ourselves, we should remember the lessons of our own education. *Learners of all ages should be taught to wrestle.* Children do not have to believe what we believe when we believe it. They can struggle with ideas on their own level and in their own way.

An old rabbinic tale has it that three rabbis were standing around, speaking of their upbringing. The first two, who had grown up in rabbinic homes, spoke about how much they had learned from their parents, and how they had carried this great knowledge into adulthood. After finishing their stories, they looked at their colleague. The third rabbi, a little embarrassed, said "You know, my father was not a rabbi. He was not even a learned man. He was a humble tailor. But he did teach me one thing: to mend what is old, and to evaluate what is new. With those words he gave me the means to become a rabbi."

If we can transmit that simple wisdom, that the past needs not to be discarded but preserved, and what is modern needs to be carefully assessed, we have given our children the tools to search on their own.

Throughout my high school and early college years, I was a pretty firm atheist. I welcomed the arguments of religious people, convinced I could knock them down. To believe in God, I thought, was an indication of weakness, an admission that one was not strong enough to face the world without a crutch.

Many of my arguments came out of my reading. Among

my favorite books were the writings of Bertrand Russell, a persuasive and witty atheist. I recall when, at seventeen and working in a Jewish summer camp, I sat on my bunk with one of the famous philosopher's books open before me. A rabbi on the staff walked over and said, "I am glad to see you are reading Bertrand Russell." Knowing how hostile Russell was to religion, I was surprised. "Why would you be glad?" I asked. "Because," the rabbi replied, "I would rather see you grow out of him than grow into him." Now it is many years later, and the rabbi has been proved right. He knew enough to realize that the struggle was not the end, but part of the process. We have to have the wisdom sometimes to plant seeds and then to wait. Our words will not always be heeded at first, but there is time.

It can be difficult to have patience in education. But even the act of not listening can at times be important to growth. As Ogden Nash wrote, "Children aren't happy without something to ignore / And that's what parents were created for."

Religion Begins in the Search. We have to keep constantly before us how important it is to give our children this ancient reservoir of wisdom, while at the same time continuing to learn ourselves. As we go along, we will discover how much family life is enhanced by religious commitment; how it provides openings for parents and children to draw close.

Embracing the search, we have to begin the task of deciding just what it is we wish our children to understand. Teaching God cannot be separated from traditions of faith. For adults who have long neglected such questions, it is best to begin with one question: What is religion all about?

WHAT RELIGION IS REALLY ABOUT

Judaism is clear: *Religion is about shaping our attitudes and actions toward ourselves, toward each other, and toward God.** *Religion should help us believe that we matter, that our actions matter, and that we are never alone.*

To believe in God is to express a certain basic confidence in what exists. Because this world was designed with people in mind, it is essentially a good world. That is the rock-bottom faith that religion can give us. This belief in the worth of the world often comes more easily to children than it does to adults. This is not only because adults have a broader experience of the problems of life, but because growing up is a process of being educated out of belief.

Adults are often the victims of their own doubtfulness. As we get older, we get less practiced at believing. When we are children, we do not yet know what is real and what is fantasy. When I was young, I believed that if I ate enough spinach (à la Popeye), I could lift up the house; that if I flapped my arms hard enough, I could fly; that monsters hid in the closet at night. Growing up is a process of shedding early illusions. So many beliefs of our early years have to be thrown away; I could not lift the house, or fly, or chase monsters from the closet. With each splash of cold truth, I grew less gullible and it became harder and harder for me to believe. Each time a belief proved false, my armor got a little

---

* Judaism contains much that does not normally fall under the category of "religion"—a land, a language, a culture, and so on. But we are here concerned primarily with the teaching of God, and although that touches all aspects of Judaism, it is especially relevant to the religious traditions of Judaism.

thicker. When I realized how much of my deep belief was just childhood imagination, I developed the "adult reflex" —skepticism.

As children, we love to be fooled. Children delight in hiding and magic tricks. How many times can a young child play hide-and-seek or "I've got your nose?" Discovering that they can be tricked is a joy to children. Riddles and mysteries do not threaten us when we are young; they charm us.

As adults, our first reaction to anything that sounds improbable is, "That can't be true." We pride ourselves on not being taken in by advertising, by false claims. After all, we are adults! Mystery is no longer charming—it is challenging. We feel we have to figure it out.

That posture forces us to be defensive. We are constantly on guard against being fooled. Even when confronted with the claims of religion, we look at them as if buying merchandise. We are wary. We are closed and suspicious.

But the need to trust goes deep. To be disenchanted with the world is to pay a terrible price. Faith does not ask us to be naive. It asks us to be confident. It asks us to trust.

So, part of our task as adults is to examine our own questions. Somewhere along the line, did we stop appreciating and trusting the world? Are we suspicious of marvels? We are trained to probe, evaluate, and measure. That is part of what it means to survive in a world where so many competing claims have to be weighed against each other. We accumulate information. Our sense of value does not always keep pace. As we grew, did we substitute certainty for wonder?

Exercise 2—Remembering What We Have Lost. Unlike other exercises in this book, this one is for adults. It can be done alone or with your spouse or friends. The exercise is to make a list of things you once believed that you no longer believe. Can you remember when you lost belief in them and why? Was it painful? The belief can be a fairy tale, like believing in Superman, or it might be political, religious, or philosophical, like believing in the goodness of all people. You may choose a personal or family belief, such as the belief in an all-wise parent. As a last step, ask yourself if you could imagine believing it again, perhaps in another form. Having completed this exercise, you might find it interesting to try it out on your children and see what beliefs they have lost along the way as well.

––––––––

Religion asks us to reopen parts of ourselves long closed. It seeks to remind us what it is to reexamine the world in order not just to understand things, but to cherish them. Faith in God begins in wonder about the world.

Religion asks those who see the world as workers to see it anew as artists. Noticing what is wonderful and allowing it to seep into our consciousness is the beginning of cultivating a sense of wonder. To understand the artist, one must take notice of the work of art.

One of the ways of finding God is to appreciate the artistry of the world together with children. Later in this book we will talk about ideas for unveiling the beauty of the world together with your children. For now let us think about renewing for ourselves an appreciation for the simple beauties that surround us.

FAITH DEMANDS GOODNESS

Religion is not only about wonder. Faith makes moral demands as well. Religion is about many things, but surely goodness is primary. To believe in the God of the Jewish tradition means to believe in a God who asks us to be good to one another. What we do in this world is the real measure of any life.

How to teach children to be good is a pressing question at any time, and never more so than today. Teaching goodness is not identical with teaching God, but they are intertwined, and neither one should be discussed alone.

What is religion? It is attitude, artistry, and action. It asks us to appreciate the world and to struggle to live decent lives. Surely this is a legacy we wish to pass on to our children.

CREATING SACRED MOMENTS

Reading a newspaper or watching a newscast inspires discussion of politics. Reading the Bible or attending synagogue inspires discussion of God.

There are many ways to open up the possibility of sacredness in our lives, and all of the ideas we discuss here can be done on many different levels. They can enrich a parent's life together with a child, a teacher's with a student. But before speaking about experiencing God with our children, we need to encourage a sense of sacredness ourselves.

The idea of reading the Bible may seem terribly remote. Most adults who return to the Bible discover, however, that it is not at all what they remember. The Bible is filled with real human beings, stories of pathos, of drama, and of depth. To study it together with a teacher or read it with a discussion group is to reenter a passionate, challenging world.

The Bible recounts the struggle of people to discover their own religiosity. We might think that every biblical hero is naturally endowed with unshakable faith. Nothing could be farther from the truth.

Consider for one moment, the story of Jacob.

※ ※ ※

Exercise 3—Reading the Bible as Adults. Instead of relying only on the following summary, you may want to try reading the story of Jacob. It is found in the book of Genesis, chapters 27–33. I recommend a translation in modern English, such as the new Jewish Publication Society translation, published under the title Tanakh. Along the way, note any questions and observations you have about the story. *Read with a critical eye.* See how many questions it raises of family dynamics, growth and change, and spirituality.

———

Jacob begins life as a trickster. He is born as a younger twin and his older brother, Esau, is slated to receive the firstborn inheritance. Jacob will not allow this to happen. Encouraged by his mother, he fools his old, blind father, Isaac. Taping animal hair on his hands so that they will feel like Esau's, he approaches his father for a blessing, claiming to be the older son. His father, suspicious but finally convinced, blesses him.

When Esau discovers that he has been cheated, he swears that as soon as his father dies, he will kill his brother. Jacob, terrified, runs away.

Many years later, after Jacob is married and has many children, he hears that his brother plans to visit him. But Esau is not coming alone. He is coming with four hundred men, and Jacob is certain that Esau intends to kill him. Jacob sends his family and entourage across the river, promising to join them the next day. The night before Esau's arrival, Jacob stands alone in the empty camp. For the first time, he is not only alone, but afraid. The text reads, "Jacob was left alone. And a man wrestled with him until the break of dawn." Who was this man who wrestled with Jacob if Jacob was indeed alone? Many commentators understand that the only person he could have been wrestling with was Jacob.

For the first time Jacob really wrestles—with who he is, with what he has done. He is beginning to grow. This is not a hero without faults. He stumbles and struggles. The next day, he goes out to meet his brother. When he does meet Esau, the two fall into each other's arms and weep.

This poignant meeting is not the end of Jacob's story. Later, he will have trouble (perhaps predictably) with his own children.* One of them, Joseph, is a dreamer. He is hated by his brothers, who end up selling him into slavery.

* To follow this part of the story, you can read Genesis, chapters 37 and 39–49.

For years Jacob thinks his son is dead and is reunited with him only at the end of his life.

As Jacob's life draws to a close, he finds himself in a foreign land, before the ruler of Egypt, the pharaoh. The pharaoh asks Jacob how old he is, to which Jacob responds, "Few and bitter have been the years of my life."

Although Jacob's life has been inordinately rich, we understand the sadness he feels now as death approaches. Surely he must cast his eye back on all the struggling he had to do to truly come to faith in God and an understanding of human relationships. It took him a long time, but his story is there so that we can learn from this honest portrayal of the conflicts and visions of one remarkable man.

The story of Jacob—so much richer than we have been able to hint at here—offers an opportunity to discuss a whole range of issues: honesty, child rearing, courage, faith, failure, God. Like the Bible as a whole, it can be read on very different levels at different ages. To children, the story of Jacob has a fairy-tale quality. As we grow, we recognize it as an honest, ageless portrait of what it means to grow in spirit.

Sadly, the most read book in history remains for many of us unopened. One of the most powerful ways adults can reopen discussions of any depth in their own lives is to read the Bible. It continues to challenge us at any age.

HOW RITUAL DRAWS US TOWARD EACH OTHER AND TOWARD GOD

The Bible is one entryway to rediscovering spirituality in our own lives. Another is the power of ritual. All religions have rituals. For we do not communicate only with words, but also with gestures and actions. Behaving a certain way can change us. *Action opens a door to feeling.* Sometimes when we are depressed we know that a new setting or a new set of behaviors will help lift the depression. It is harder to be depressed while dancing than while sitting in a dark room. The act itself carries our heart with it.

If you want to change how you feel, change what you do. This commonsense wisdom about mood is equally true when it comes to our approach to God.

When candles are lit for the Sabbath, it changes the atmosphere of the house and the feel of the evening. Suddenly there is a sense of sanctity. It is a simple act to light candles. The traditional Hebrew blessing is only fourteen words. Yet the moment is magical. When in my childhood my mother stood before the two candles, reciting the blessing, the room was transformed. The action opened a path among members of the family and between us and God.

Adults who have so many other rituals in their lives sometimes forget religious ritual. They get dressed a certain way, read the morning newspaper in a designated spot, and never fail to catch a particular TV show. It helps to standardize life. Rituals and habits help to order the world.

But religious ritual also helps to order the world. It helps us to understand who we are and our place in things. In the middle of a complicated life, ritual reminds us what is important, why we are here, our direction. Each morning the Jewish prayer service prompts us to ask simple, basic questions: Who are we? What is our life? What is the sum of our actions? We are trying to figure out the importance of what we do. The more deeply we have a grasp on ourselves, the more powerful an image of adulthood we can pass on to our children. Ritual not only orders the world; it opens doors to self-understanding.

Ritual also opens the doors to communication with God. Each act is an opening, because it gives us a moment to feel a sense of sanctity in our lives. Holiness is a need that does not disappear with the passing years.

When we are young we often assume that childhood needs will one day vanish. We may need to feel holiness, awe, and comfort when we are young. Yet something convinces us that as adults we will outgrow these emotions.

One of the shocking discoveries of growing up is that growing up never quite happens. When we are children, we expect there will be a magical moment one morning when we shall climb out of the bed and suddenly be adults. All the inadequacies and uncertainties will melt away in the morning sunlight, and we will be like those confident adults we envy from afar.

The transformation never takes place. We have learned to disguise or suppress certain needs, but they still exist. We carry within us all that we have been. Just as we needed holiness as children, we need holiness—deeper, more thoughtful, but essentially the same—as adults.

There is no age limit on the drive for sanctity. Even as

adults, we need something greater than ourselves in our lives.

Ritual can make us uncomfortable, self-conscious. But that is true of most things that stretch us. The first time we stumble through a dance or try a new sport, we find that our bodies can be awkward and unused to the activity. It takes a long time before we learn enough of a foreign language to speak even a single sentence without hesitation and discomfort. The body develops its own pathways, its own memory. Given enough practice, one day, swinging a tennis racket or speaking French will be second nature.

The same is true of religious ritual. At first it may feel clumsy. Reciting blessings might be unnatural to us, especially if we did not grow up with them. But in time we discover that there is a rhythm and a grace to it, just as there is in athletics. Gradually we learn. In time we develop our own particular manner of practicing the ritual, and our individual customs become special to us as well.

Friday night dinner in my parents' home is a good example. To open Sabbath dinner, we recited the blessing on the wine and then the blessing of the bread, the challah. This is a standard Jewish practice. In most homes the bread is then sliced and gently distributed. My father was not so genteel with his challah. Pieces were tossed—really, thrown—around the table, and all of us had to catch our own slice. That was the only time food was thrown in my house. Only for that tradition would my mother permit it. The throwing became almost as much a part of the ritual as the recitation of the blessing—and it was more fun. Immediately after the bread, my father would bless each of us in the traditional manner. Now as an adult, the entire ritual means even more to me than it did as a child. It touches something deep inside me—a family memory and a sense that we were so at home with the ritual that we could give it our own twist, and still it was sacred. It ties together the warmth of family, the liveliness of the game, and a moment of holiness.

Things need not be solemn to be sacred. Joy goes well with holiness, and laughter enhances the sacred. One Talmudic rabbi goes so far as to say, "There is no sadness in the presence of God."

Practicing ritual does take time and effort. Not every instant will be magical. But even when the moment is less than wondrous, it serves a purpose. The theologian Abraham Joshua Heschel tells the story of a town where all the clocks stopped. Despite the best efforts of the townspeople, none of the clocks could be coaxed into starting again. Eventually the people of the town gave up and let their timepieces stand and rust. But one man wound his clock every day, just as he had when it ran. One day a watchmaker happened to pass through town. The clocks that had been neglected were now so rusty, they were beyond repair. But the watch that had been wound each day could be fixed. So it is, says Heschel, with our religious impulse, our sense of God—it needs constant winding. The time will come when it will run on its own.

Ritual is how we wind our spiritual clocks. At first it feels awkward. Then it feels good. Finally it feels indispensable.

Exercise 4—Experimenting with Ritual. Together with your children, pick a ritual to observe as a sort of "tryout." You might try lighting candles each Friday night. Or blessing bread before a meal. Or thanking God together each morning for a new day. (See the appendix for examples. You can get many more ideas from some of the books listed in the bibliography.) Whichever ritual you choose, the key is to choose it together. This is a family ritual.

———

Finding our own way to faith is the best possible beginning to helping children. It is not the only way. We often say, "You cannot give what you do not have," but that is not really true. You can give reassurance when you yourself are scared, comfort when shaken, and even faith when you doubt. The key is not to take your own faith and transplant it into the soul of a child. The key is to take what you have —your own faith, questions, ideas, even doubts—and use them to enable the child to develop his or her own way.

DOES RELIGION GIVE OUR CHILDREN ROOM TO BE CREATIVE?

As parents have discovered throughout history, our children's way might not be precisely our own. That is not a new problem. Judaism has an extraordinary history. For thousands of years there have been Jews whose practices and ideas often varied. There are certain beliefs and constants. Still, there are many different ways to be Jewish. In reexamining our own roots, in encouraging our kids, we should not confine ourselves to the specifics we learned as children.

There is an old tale about two men who studied with the same rabbi. Growing up, both of them learned his ways and followed his teachings with care. In time they separated, and many years passed. One day they met again. The first student faithfully kept to all the teachings of his master. All the practices he had learned, he still repeated. All the explanations he had been taught, he still believed.

The second student had changed. Over time his own ideas had developed, and he had discovered the interpretations of others. His practice was now quite different from that of his revered teacher. The first disciple was disappointed with his friend. "Why," he asked, "have you gone astray? Wasn't what you learned good enough for you? Why don't you follow the teachings of our master?"

His friend answered, "But I have followed him. In fact, I followed our master better than you. For you see, our rabbi grew up and left his teacher. Now I have grown up and left mine."

That story reminds us that we are not faithful only when we imitate. We can also be faithful when we create. We need to remember that for ourselves, as we rediscover what our faith means to us. We also need to remember that for our children, as they seek to take our teachings and make them their own.

We should beware how much authority we have as adults and how easily it can be misused. The idea is to stimulate discovery, not to lay down unchanging laws for children to follow slavishly. Our authority over our own children is fleeting. And teachers know that an idea does not stick unless students can be prompted to uncover it for themselves.

To me, the shakiness of authority will always be symbolized by Crest toothpaste. When I was a very young child, my mother bought Crest toothpaste. I never saw another brand in my house. I gradually developed the idea that nothing else one could put on one's teeth was as effective, as good—as virtuous. When I visited a friend's house and saw they used another toothpaste, I wondered how uninformed, or just uncaring, their parents must be. It seemed to me that everyone who loved their children must know enough to use Crest.

As I got a bit older, I discovered that it was possible to be wise, to love one's children, and yet use Colgate. My world was shaken. Colgate! Even Pepsodent! What else, I wondered, that my parents had taught me as a child was similarly up for grabs?

In the years since then it has become clear to me how much of our lives is about holding fast to such beliefs, some with more reason, some with less. When one of these beliefs is changed, it threatens to explode much that we care about. Simple things like what toothpaste we use can be a test case for the worthiness of other beliefs we are taught. Silly things often serve as powerful symbols. To me, toothpaste was an emblem of my parents' good judgment.

That is one reason to let children have some room. Not all beliefs have equal weight. Teaching well means giving room for questioning without fearing that questions will undermine everything. When we stake too much on any single belief, we are inviting our children to find out we are wrong and so discredit all we believe in.

HOW MUCH WE TEACH WITHOUT KNOWING IT

One of the important messages in that story is that my parents were never aware of how important toothpaste was to me. As children we entertain beliefs, conclusions, and fantasies that others do not know. So as parents we have to be aware that many of the messages we intend to transmit are not those our children receive.

Much of our education is unintended. Much of it is also unanticipated. We never know where important messages will come from. Education happens in the margins of life, in the casual remark and in the small incident. We are teaching at every moment, whether we want to or not. The only question is what we will teach. What children remember is often quite different from what we planned.

That is why teaching religion must be done not in careful, specified settings, but all the time. Faith must be lived. The disciple of a famous rabbi traveled for miles to be in the presence of his teacher. When asked why he had traveled so far, he said it was not to hear the rabbi's formal lessons, but to see how he tied his shoelaces. Not merely what we say, but our daily actions carry our true teachings. As in the old phrase, "Faith is not just taught, but caught." We never know when the message will seep into the heart.

Education does not come with guarantees. All we can do is keep the issue alive. We can create openings for discussion, for shared experiences. We can teach and listen. When the great rabbi Menachem Mendel of Kotzk was asked by his disciples how he became a follower of the Chasidic movement, he told them that in his town there was an old man who used to tell stories.

"Those stories," said the rabbi, "persuaded me."

One of his students commented that to move someone so much the old storyteller must have been a great teacher, a great scholar.

"No," said the rabbi, "he was a simple storyteller. But he told what he knew, and I heard what I needed."

All children, even those from nonreligious homes, develop images of God. It is our responsibility to help them develop those ideas in a way that is constructive and true both to traditions we value and to what we know about the world. We can tell only what we know and hope they hear what they need. In what follows we will try to figure out how to talk with children about religion in general, about God, about goodness, about death. Passing on that wisdom is a parenting and teaching task we cannot ignore. It is a task requiring not only skill, but spirit.

QUESTIONS TO DISCUSS
WITH YOUR CHILDREN

1. Do you ever talk about God in school?

2. What have you heard about God from your friends?

3. What does it feel like when we light candles?

4. Do you think about God? When?

5. Are there questions about God you would like to ask me?

Catching It from Our Kids:
How Do They See the World, and
What Can We Learn from Them?

The Maggid (storyteller) of Dubnov once explained how important the spirituality of children was to adults. He told the following parable:

Once there was a father who traveled with his son for miles. Each time they reached an obstacle such as a river or mountain, the father lifted his son on his shoulders and carried him through the difficult terrain. Finally they came to their destination—a walled castle. But the gate of the castle was shut up, and there were only narrow windows on the sides of the wall. The father said to his son: "My son, up until now I have carried you. Now the only way we can reach our destination is if you will climb through the windows, and open the gate for me from within."

So it is, said the Maggid, with parents and children and God. Parents take care of their children, feed and clothe them, and see them through all sorts of obstacles. Yet parents who have so many strengths, often find the gate to God closed. But children have a special spiritual magic. They can climb to places their parents cannot reach. Children can fling open the gates of heaven from within so that they and their parents can reach God together.

ADULTS NEED TO find a way to learn about faith. One place to look for that learning is to our children. Teaching is a two-way process, and as we begin teaching, we should prepare to begin learning.

We sometimes forget how much the special perspective of children can help foster our own faith. Children remind us that it is important not only to understand the world, but to cherish it.

To share their appreciation, we have to be able to encourage our children to tell us their thoughts and ideas. As parents we need to learn how to ask. We need to be able to be silent and listen. Often there is magic in the answers we will hear. Our part of the exchange is to assure our children that their ideas matter and are worthy.

We give our children a sense of their own worthiness in many ways. None of those ways is more important than reminding them that they are created in the image of God. Being created in God's image makes a person invaluable. As adults we can see God's image in the faces of these new lives that we created, lives entrusted to us.

Part of the magic of being around children is seeing how much they have to show us. Children's intensity, their ability to dwell in the moment, their capacity for joy—all of this helps us to "catch it from our kids."

———

According to Jewish lore, the prophet Elijah will arrive during the Passover seder meal to announce the coming of the Messiah. At the beginning of the meal, a cup of wine is placed at the center of the table. There the wine stands, the "cup of Elijah," waiting for the prophet's appearance. During the meal, the door is opened in ceremonial welcome.

In my parents' home, we observed the familiar custom of having the youngest child open the door. Each year my younger brother, Danny, was charged with the task. As he grew up, he took this task seriously, feeling the importance of his assignment.

What Danny also learned as he grew older was that solemn religious moments provide some of the best opportunities for family teasing and pranks. One year, one of my older brothers, Paul, waited outside and walked right in when Danny opened the door. Danny was shocked. The next year, Danny made sure that all of us were safely around the table before opening the door. However, Paul had placed our dog right outside, and the dog came charging through the door. Once again, Danny was completely taken aback.

The following year, amid laughter and joking warnings, Danny made sure that every living thing in the Wolpe household was safely inside. This time Paul had leaned a broom up against the door so that it fell in when the door was opened.

Detailing the practical jokes played against my younger brother is not the point of this story. Rather, the key is that the next year Paul did nothing. Danny opened the door and all was silent. We had not given up on all practical jokes, but this one no longer had a point. As long as Danny was young enough to expect Elijah, we could startle him. Now he had grown too old to believe that Elijah might really walk in the door. He no longer anticipated redemption and so could no longer really be shocked by dogs, or brooms, or brothers. The belief in Elijah's return was a special kind of hope. For Danny, that hope was gone.

He was losing faith. He was becoming an adult.

There is sadness in losing the beliefs of childhood. Something invaluable slips away that will never return. Some of it cannot be helped. We cannot continue to believe in fantasies.

But sometimes we lose things that we *could* hold on to. Contact with children can remind us that growing up is not only shedding illusion. If we are not careful, growing up can mean losing the capacity to hope or neglecting to notice that the world is charged with magic. The time must come when we no longer believe in the tooth fairy, but the time need never come when we forget that the tooth fairy symbolizes certain miracles: the miracle of growth and change; the miracle of parental love.

That is why Jewish tradition holds that the Passover seder cannot be completed without children. They are needed not only to open doors. A central part of the seder is the search for the *afikomen,* and it is children who must find this bit of matzoh that concludes the seder. The leader of the seder hides it, and the children search. When the children finally come up with the *afikomen,* they hold it for "ransom." They can use the *afikomen* to bargain for gifts and sweets, for without that matzoh the seder is unfinished. Since the seder tells the story of redemption from the land of Egypt, we understand that children hold in their hands the key to redemption. And since redemption in the future is the great goal of history in Judaism, the lesson is clear: Children are at the center of what adults yearn for and need.

In that sense, Danny's early belief was right. He did have something to do with redemption, with salvation. Without children, no tradition can endure. When he opened the door, performing an act that had been performed by children for generations, it was just as important as he understood it to be. Despite the teasing of older brothers, Danny's seriousness was closer to the truth than our skepticism.

When the prophet Isaiah, in a famous image of redemption, speaks of the lion lying down with the lamb, he concludes: "And a little child shall lead them" (Isa. 11:6).

LEARNING TO BECOME A FOOL—CAN CHILDREN HELP US BE CHILDLIKE?

Children bring us perspectives that enrich us if we are clever enough to pay attention. There is a lovely talmudic tale of a man whose father died and left a very strange provision in his will. The will gave everything to this only child, his son. But the gift was conditional. It said the son could not inherit "until he became a fool."

The man consulted Rabbi Jose and Rabbi Judah, neither of whom could figure out the meaning of the provision. They went to confer with Rabbi Joshua ben Karcha. They saw him outside his house, crawling on his hands and knees with a reed in his mouth, playing with his child.

When they explained the will, Rabbi Joshua laughed and said: "What you just saw is your answer." The will meant he could not inherit until he had children. Children allow us to become fools again. They pull us away from our weighty adult concerns and bring us closer to God. Taking children seriously means coming out of ourselves, out of our distance, and rediscovering parts of the world we left behind.

⊠ ⊠ ⊠

Exercise 1—Becoming a Fool. This exercise is to bring us out of ourselves. The goal is simple—to act like a fool with your children. Try inventing a nonsense language and speaking it to each other for one afternoon. Or play a game like Monopoly but make up rules as you go along. Or sing (or even better, whistle) "The Star-Spangled Banner" staring at each other—and the first one to laugh loses. Shed some seriousness. The pursuit of spirituality can be loose and easy; it need not always be somber.

———

Children help us discover not only the wonder of the world, but the wonder of ourselves. Things we take for granted—eating, talking, walking—become new again as we watch another human being acquire these skills. We realize again what a marvel it is to be a person. The Jewish tradition expresses this by teaching that we are all in the image of God.

THE MIRACLE OF YOU

The primary miracle that children discover and share is themselves. As adults we take for granted that we dwell in a certain body, that we are who we are. As children, our very being is a miracle.

We seemed marvelous to ourselves when we were children. Every sense was an adventure; seeing things, touching things, thinking, and speaking were not taken for granted.

In our children that sense of astonishment at human functioning is alive today. And this sense of amazement does not belong to children alone. It is shared by the religious spirit. God has made us glorious. As the psalmist writes: "You have made me a little lower than the angels, and crowned me with glory and honor" (Ps. 8). To be human is to be almost divine, a wondrous creation.

Of all created beings, the Torah tells us, human beings were made last. Why? Because, the Talmud adds in explanation, just as a host wishes first to prepare everything for the feast and then to bring in the honored guest, God wanted all to be ready for people before ushering them into the world.

Such tales remind us that how we regard ourselves is crucial. There is no crime more serious, runs an old Jewish teaching, than letting ourselves forget that we are royalty. We must constantly recall our own dignity. That dignity is awakened by seeing the astonishment in a child's eyes when he figures out something new about the way he works, or walks, or thinks. Then the trick becomes understanding and encouraging that blossoming sense of self.

Having a child can open a parent's eyes to the idea that a person is in the image of God. Parents then have a responsibility to teach their children what they have learned from their children—they are the image of God in this world. The Midrash (rabbinic commentary) says that in the formation of each child are three partners: a man, a woman, and

God. In other words, we carry inside not only the genetic impress of our parents, but also the spiritual impress of God. When we restrict a child's world to two partners, we rob him of the most exalted compliment—that he is in the image of God.

EXPLAINING THE MEANING OF "THE IMAGE OF GOD"

What does it mean to be in the image of God? Clearly it is not a physical image, because God has no body. Sometimes we think that it must mean that human beings have intellects. Yet we would not say that a person with a higher IQ is more in God's image than another. We cannot find the Divine in any single ability. The bit of God inside of us is not in our capacities—not in our ability to speak or to reason or even to love, although all of these may play some part.

The image of God is precisely that part of the person we cannot point to or name. The spark of the Divine is that which makes you unmistakably you. When we insist to our children that they are in God's image, we are telling them something about their uniqueness. It is not something they can measure—not their ability to speak, or to understand, or even to love. It is that spark which makes them who they are. It is the soul they carry within.

"There are no doubles," said the great rabbi the Baal Shem Tov. He meant that there were no two identical moments, identical insights, identical people. Everything has a special slant, because God did not put the same bit of godliness into any two people, no matter how alike they may seem. Each child is unique.

To some, that uniqueness is a result of heredity. To Judaism it is a result of divinity.

▩ ▩ ▩

Exercise 2—Whom Do You See in the Mirror? According to theologian Abraham Joshua Heschel, we should not *make* images of God in this world (idols) because we *are* images of God. Can we see that in ourselves?

Have your child look in the mirror with you. See if you can both pick out features that you took from someone else —hair or eyes or lips or nose from one parent or grandparent. Then see if you can get a sense of the sparkle that comes not from any genetic inheritance, but from God. Do you see it in your eyes? In the light of your smile? Can you see God in yourself, and in each other?

———

The sense of awe that children have about themselves can bring us back to this central fact. A child who is fascinated by his own form is not being childish. He is exploring the magnificent art of God and the bit of God that is inside him.

Adults should be touched by that realization. And we should foster it. Each child has a right to know that he or she is created in God's image.

CAN THE BELIEF THAT WE ARE IN GOD'S IMAGE HELP OUR SELF-ESTEEM?

Self-esteem is a popular topic in lectures and books these days. We are told that it is important for all to develop a sense of self-worth. True self-esteem goes much deeper than being good at some activity or skilled in schoolwork, important as those may be.

There are many ways that a child can feel important. Like their parents, children tend to think first of special things they can do or how others feel about them. We may think ourselves important because we are handsome or pretty; because we have nice parents or husbands or wives; because we are good at our jobs or at study or at sports.

The great problem with this is that all the reasons listed in the previous paragraph can change. Looks and jobs are fleeting. Husbands and wives do not always stay beside each other. All accomplishment, though we hope it lasts and seek to hold on to it, is never without the possibility of change. Anything that is human is temporary, and if our most basic level of self-esteem is founded on that which can change, so will our sense of ourselves.

Instead, our self-esteem should be grounded in something permanent. An important legacy to give our children is just the sort of permanent sense of self-esteem we seek for ourselves. *If we are in the image of God, we are always important. We will have good days and bad, successes and failures, but we will never be worthless. We are invaluable.* There is no richer soil in which to plant self-esteem.

CAN SELF-ESTEEM MAKE US FEEL BAD?

That we are in God's image grants a sense of importance and a sense of responsibility. One of the mistakes we make about self-esteem is to think that it always translates into feeling good about yourself. Quite the opposite. Sometimes to have self-esteem means to feel bad. It means to realize that you did not do what you were capable of doing. People who see themselves as great artists will be bothered by a minor mistake in their art. Great athletes are upset with performances that are beneath their high standards. And people who believe themselves really worthwhile will be upset when they forsake the godliness inside of them.

Rabbi Abraham Twerski writes that when his father wanted to reprimand him, he would not say, "What you did was bad." Instead he would say, "What you did was not worthy of you." The beginning of a father's reprimand was acknowledgment of his child's importance.

In the Talmud, the rabbis contrast a human king, who mints coins, with the Divine King, who fashions people. The coins all look alike, but each human face is different. To be a person is to be unrepeatable. In that same passage we are told that to save one individual is equivalent to saving an entire world. Each person is a whole world, because each has been given infinite worth by God. Each person is a whole world because each bears a unique essence. No greater gift can be given to a child than that assurance.

Children do not only allow us to act like fools, they also teach us to take ourselves seriously.

HOW CAN CHILDREN TEACH US THE IMPORTANCE OF THE PRESENT?

One of the demands of religion is that we not lose what exists in contemplation of what might be. Too often we cannot appreciate what is happening now, because we are too busy contemplating the past with regret or the future with anticipation. As a result, the world slips by us. Here, too, our children can teach us. Again it is not an intellectual lesson; it is, rather, something we "catch" from our kids.

Children know how to focus on the tasks at hand. They appreciate the great truth that the future will come regardless of our worrying and that the greatest impact (as well as the most fun) is to be had in the present.

One writer speaks about having learned a great lesson from watching a child build a sand castle on the beach. The child spent all day carefully constructing the sand castle. Bit by bit, he fashioned the moat and the towers. As he was completing the whole structure, the tide rose and wiped it all away. The child shrugged his shoulders. The next day he was out building again. The moment, the doing, was of capital importance. What happened later did not steal the value of time already filled.

The Talmud makes the remark that the learning of a child is like writing on fresh paper. A later rabbi, commenting on that statement, says that "fresh paper" implies that children can concentrate on what they are learning at the moment. They are not distracted by clutter on the page. Few sights are as remarkable as young faces in concentration, intent on what is before them. The paper is fresh, and the moment is alive.

That power to be absorbed and delighted can also teach us. A connection to God begins in the appreciation of God's overwhelming world. We respect a scientist who studies the tiniest vein in a flower in order to understand it. There is no less intensity in a child who traces the vein with his finger in order to appreciate it. Collecting pinecones is an act of devotion. We can catch the devotion and turn it toward God.

For adults to ignore the distractions of the day is difficult. The phone rings; work beckons; the TV is a button away. Yet the child can sit among all this in the middle of the floor, engrossed by a shoebox. There is a quality of attention that is precious because it is not directed toward any goal. Children do not study shoeboxes to manufacture better boxes. They study them because they *are*. That is a rare but wonderful devotion. It is important and necessary to study things for some purpose. It is holy to study them for no purpose. Each moment is precious not because of what it can be used for, but simply because it is. Creation is only one use of time. Another is appreciation.

Appreciation happens in the present. Children constantly pull us from our wanderings in the future, or our memories of the past, to the ground of "now." Is there any sentence the child repeats more often than "Now"? I recall watching a child walking with his mother, repeatedly insisting, "Now," to which his mother kept responding, "Later." After a few such exchanges, the child said, "Now *is* later."

When his teacher died, the rabbi of Kotzk was asked what was most important to his teacher. "Whatever he was doing at the moment," was the reply. Children, who have an inexhaustible capacity for caring deeply about the "now," can remind us of this critical fact. They know intuitively what the sophisticated philosopher Alfred North Whitehead arrived at after years of reflection: "The present is holy ground."

Are Our Children Normal Mystics?

There are only two ways to live your life. One is as though nothing is a miracle. The other is as though everything is a miracle.

Albert Einstein

A scholar once spoke about the way the rabbis of the Talmud saw the world as "normal mysticism." It was not mysticism in the way we often think of it: it did not involve fantastic visions or souls flying off to other worlds. It was not the sort of mysticism that required endless hours of meditation. The rabbis went about their business on a daily basis. They practiced trades, fixed shoes, sold goods, and studied, but at each moment their consciousness was charged with a sense of God's presence.

A normal mystic sees the closeness of God always reflected in the world. Just as a person looking at a painting "reads" the personality of the artist, the normal mystic gets a glimpse of God's nature by looking at the world.

When children have a particular sense of God, it often has to do with their attitude toward the world around them. Someone who grows up on a farm has a different sense of creation, and therefore of God, from one who grows up on the streets of a city. The simple act of looking at the sky at night and seeing stars—something the city dweller can rarely do—influences a person's ideas about who we are and where we come from. The stars at night, the sky in the day, the sight of people bustling on a crowded street, can say something about the force behind and beyond the world.

We can reawaken our own faculty of noticing the world by seeing it through the eyes of our children. We drive to work the same route each day and see nothing. But if we bring a child in the car, that child can fix on something wonderful. As often as not, it is children who carry out the advice of the naturalist John Burroughs: "If you wish to see something new, take the same walk you took yesterday." We can take the same walk, and if we only pay attention each time, the world will present a new angle of its familiar dress.

▣ ▣ ▣

Exercise 3—Noticing God's World. This exercise is a familiar one—a nature walk. But it does not have to be done in the forest. You can walk around any neighborhood, or even in your backyard. You are looking for wonders that God has created. It could be insects, grass, stones—anything. Do not forget that children are a couple of feet closer to the ground, and they may naturally notice things that we have long since literally "outgrown."

A companion to this is to keep a "wonder table." That is a place where children can display wonders they have found, like pinecones or seashells or birds' nests. Feel the depth of their natural awe for these everyday wonders.

I once asked children in a class of mine to draw a picture of God. One child drew a picture of a wizard spinning the world on his finger like a basketball. When I asked him to explain his picture, he told me that he always saw God's face peering down at us, like the wizard in the picture. In his picture it was clearly a kind face and a warm image.

This child had taken two steps. First, he saw the world as wizardry. It held marvels for him, and he took note of them. Second, he saw each marvel as reflecting back to God.

A normal mystic seeks to see the world in this way all the time. Most of us can reach the state of catching glimpses of God only in certain moments. Even when we are trained to see the world that way, we sometimes forget. The poet Robert Frost was once having dinner with a young lady as the sun was setting.

"Oh, look, Mr. Frost," she said, "the sunset is so beautiful."

"I'm sorry," Frost replied, "but I make it a rule not to talk shop during dinner."

Part of Frost's joke is to remind us that even poets do not always have the power to appreciate. The artistry of the world slips away from everyone at times, through fatigue or inattention. The trick is to try to create moments of awareness as often as possible. Watch the natural normal mystics—children—and learn from them.

IN SEARCHING FOR GOD,
WE CHANGE OURSELVES

There is a wonderful Chasidic story about the child of a
rabbi who used to wander in the woods. At first his father
let him wander, but over time he became concerned. The
woods were dangerous. The father did not know what
lurked there.

He decided to discuss the matter with his child. One day
he took him aside and said, "You know, I have noticed that
each day you walk into the woods. I wonder, why do you
go there?"

The boy said to his father, "I go there to find God."

"That is a very good thing," the father replied gently. "I
am glad you are searching for God. But, my child, don't you
know that God is the same everywhere?"

"Yes," the boy answered, "but I'm not."

When we undertake a search for God, it often involves
changing our setting and our mind-set. We have to find a
place that allows us to seek.

Sometimes, as in the story of this child, the setting
will be geographical. But to be a normal mystic one does
not have to live in a forest. Instead, we have to take the
normal occurrences of life and change the way we look at
them. We have to turn them upward—refer them back
to God.

The Jewish tradition is filled with examples of blessings.
When we bless something special in this world, we seek to
connect not only to God, but to a specific part of ourselves.

We try to connect to that which will allow us to view the world with the dimension of holiness.

Some blessings are standard, such as the blessing recited when we eat bread. Such prayer formulas cover repeated, daily events. Others help us to take note of our world. They are blessings we recite when seeing something that stands out in nature or among people. Instead of merely noting how marvelous they are, we see them as "normal mystics" —by blessing God for their existence, we remind ourselves of God's presence in the world.

- Upon trying a new food, wearing new clothes, or celebrating a significant moment in life, we express our gratitude toward God: *Blessed are You, Lord our God, King of the Universe, Who has kept us in life, sustained us, and enabled us to reach this day.*
- Upon seeing the wonders of nature, particularly those that are awe-inspiring, we turn our appreciation to God, who created the world: *Blessed are You, Lord our God, King of the Universe, who creates the world.*

There are many other blessings contained in the Jewish tradition: for seeing a rainbow, on seeing the ocean, upon encountering leaders or scholars, and many more. All attest to the connection the tradition makes between the wonder of the world and the glory of God. It is training in being a normal mystic.

Blessings like these help us to pause and acknowledge special moments. At times the most special moments are those that are repeated each day. Bedtime offers a repeated opportunity to open up worlds inside of ourselves, worlds we get to glimpse because we are led there by our children.

Nighttime intensifies awareness of the mystery of things. Prayers at bedtime are traditional. The current that runs between parents and children saying prayers together in the night is unique. Reciting the Shema (see appendix), the Hebrew prayer customarily said upon retiring, or even a simple blessing, can deepen bonds in a special way. The night gives the world a shadowy wonder, the sort of atmosphere out of which devotion is born.

※ ※ ※

Exercise 4—Writing Your Own Blessing. Together with your child, write your own blessing thanking God for something precious in your life. You don't have to stick to any formula. The key is to make sure that it is a blessing the child initiates and to remember to recite it together.

———

As children awaken a sense of wonder in us, we can teach them how to refer that wonder back to God, how to give their appreciation a spiritual dimension. To say that something is beautiful is a fine beginning. We want to go further: to see it as part of the great artwork of the universe and God as the Divine artist. Having taken those steps, we have touched the realm of the normal mystic; we move beyond appreciation, to sanctity.

HOW DOES YOUR CHILD SEE
THE WORLD?

Adults have spent years pulling together a vision of the world. We see the world in our own way. It is easy to forget how differently our children can see the same things. Asking children how they see the world can produce some surprising results. The messages children receive are often not the ones we think we are sending. The sort of reversal that children can practice on our thinking confounds and delights us. An often repeated story is of the child who was drawing a picture with intense concentration. His mother asked him what he was doing.

"I'm drawing a picture of God," he said.

"But," his mother protested, "no one knows what God looks like."

The child looked up proudly. "Well, they will when I'm finished!"

The messages we seek to transmit are not always the ones our children receive. Telling the child in the story above that no one knows what God looks like was seen not as a fact, but as a challenge. In the following story, we realize that our literal message is often very different from our intended message.

I was serving as a student rabbi in a synagogue, and one night the senior rabbi, Moshe Rothblum, began to tell a story. It was a Friday family Sabbath, and the seats were filled with children. Rabbi Rothblum is an animated storyteller, and he had the children on the edge of their seats.

There was a couple, he said, who were lying in bed at

night, and the window was open and it was very cold. Each one wanted the other to get up and close the window. After arguing about who should get up to close the window, they struck a deal—whoever talked first had to close the window.

They lay in silence. The room grew colder and colder, but each was stubborn and refused to go over and close the window. An hour passed.

In time they heard a stirring downstairs. A burglar had broken into the house. They continued to lie silently. The burglar calmly gathered up all their possessions, but still neither one spoke. Silver was being dumped into a bag, other possessions knocked over and broken, but the two kept quiet. In a short time, the entire house was ransacked. Still, neither one would speak.

Upon leaving, the burglar dropped his cigarette on the living room rug. Smoke began to rise through the house. It got hotter and hotter. Finally flames burst through the bedroom door. The husband cried out, "Fire!"

His wife, triumphant, said, "Aha! Now you have to close the window."

Rabbi Rothblum finished the story to the laughter of the adults. He said to the children, "Now, can anyone tell me the moral of that story?"

A little girl smack in the center of the congregation jumped up, waving her hand wildly. "It shows," said the little girl, "that if you want something badly enough, and you try hard enough, in the end you'll get it."

Her reading of the story made a certain kind of sense. It was a literal reading that was, in its way, beyond an adult to capture. Certainly it was not the message the adults in the congregation thought the rabbi was giving.

Anyone who has children, or who has worked with children, is filled with such stories. They show a continuing process of working on and evaluating the world, which can have remarkable results.

HOW DO WE DISCOVER
OUR CHILDREN'S WORLDVIEW?

Naturally much of this will be hidden from us if we do not ask. As adults, we are used to being asked. We are always being asked by children to explain this or that or to tell them why. As often as not, to turn around and ask for *their* theories first can have a stunning effect. Instead of being so involved in our framing of the answer, we should encourage their framing of the question. Just like adults, children sometimes ask a question in order to tell you something about their own ideas.

"Do you know why God made it so Moses couldn't speak right?" asked Jeremy.

"Why?" I said.

"So people like my sister wouldn't feel so bad."

That led to a long discussion of Jeremy's sister's speech impediment and how Moses' having a speech impediment made him realize what Jeremy's sister could achieve. Jeremy's question was not about interpreting the biblical text. A question can be a pretext to open discussion.

To ask a child a question is to open a door. Inside is a miscellany, filled with colorful bits, with fears and fantasies. If we don't ask, the door remains closed.

When a child asks where the world comes from, offering a long, proper explanation may just dampen what is to come. I remember Marty, an eight-year-old student in Hebrew school who had just heard about evolution from his science teacher. He was not yet too clear on the details, and he asked me what I thought happened. Sensing that something was brewing, I asked him what *he* thought.

Marty explained to me that one day a big fish had been chasing a little fish. He ran around the room, showing the frantic movements of the little fish who was being chased. Finally the little fish was being overtaken. There was nowhere for him to go. In desperation, he swam so fast toward the shore that he popped out of the water and landed on the ground. The big fish did not dare to follow him there, and life on earth was born.

It would have been easy to explain what was wrong with this theory. Soon, no doubt, Marty would find out that the process had to be a bit less immediate. Nonetheless, the idea itself was a perfect opportunity to understand Marty's basic vision of the world, how things came to be, and whether God could fit into that picture.

Indeed, when I asked Marty if God could fit into his picture, it was clear he had already thought about it. He explained patiently (sometimes children treat their elders like idiots, and I suppose sometimes they are right) that of course God was involved. After all, a fish alone could not breathe on dry land, so God must have sustained that first fish so that it could grow and give birth to other fish who would survive.

I saw that Marty had an idea of God as caregiving and concerned. Had I "answered" his question about evolution, all of that would have been buried under my careful answer.

Exercise 5—Learning Your Children's Theories. This is less an exercise than a suggestion for a continuing practice. As you work through this book, asking your children for their theories will yield constantly interesting results. The questions at the end of this and other chapters are to aid in this.

———————

DO WE TELL ALL WE KNOW?

At times facts have to be withheld so that imaginations can pour forth. I am not recommending that we shield children from facts, but the decision of when to tell something is as important as what we tell.

Adults accumulate an enormous amount of information, and imaginations can get buried under all the facts. The late Nobel Prize–winning scientist Richard Feynman once even speculated that great scientific discoveries were made mostly by young scientists because they did not yet know too much! Once they were older, their judgment was better, but their creativity lessened. There is no doubt that as adults we have to be careful to withhold as well as to give.

One of the perils of growing up is forgetting how authoritative adults can sound to children. Even if the child argues and objects, for a while, at least, an answer carries an almost unimaginable weight of persuasive power. If we are too quick with our answers, and too overwhelming with our facts, discussion will get lost in lectures. Our knowledge is important for children to recognize and learn from. But if we exercise it too freely, not only do we block our children's ideas, but we never get to learn from them.

LISTENING AND QUESTIONING

So insistent are children's questions that they are easy to turn off or to ignore. The "why"'s can be endless. Nonetheless, probing their questions patiently can yield priceless insights.

Listening to children's questions, finding out what they are really asking, and inviting them to address it themselves are three steps that can help draw out their own ideas. All too often we are so intent on proving our own worthiness as parents and guides that we jump in with answers. We do not want to be thought of as less than omniscient.

The fear that we will be found less than knowledgeable leads us into mistakes. How many times have we told a child something incorrect because we were afraid of not knowing the answer? We would have been better off listening to the question, understanding it well, and asking for the child's theories. A teacher's role is not solely to provide answers. Often it is more important to understand the question and the questioner. As with Jeremy asking about Moses and his speech impediment, the question is often about something other than what it appears at first. Jeremy was asking so that I would understand *him* better.

We do not encourage questions by always knowing the "correct" response. As the Talmud reminds us, each person should teach his tongue to say "I don't know."

We not only want to ask our children questions to understand their perspective; we want to encourage them to ask questions of others as well. The Nobel Prize–winning physicist I. I. Rabi once told an interviewer that his most important intellectual influence was his mother. Each day when Rabi came home from school, his mother would say to him, "Isaac, did you ask any good questions today?" From that, said Rabi, he learned that the key to life was to ask good questions.

Encouraging children to ask questions, seeking to understand their worldview, trying to catch their wonder for the world—these can help in our quest for God and can help better train our kids to look for God in their lives.

What can we catch from our kids? The recognition that hope is an act of piety, not of gullibility. A renewed realization that each moment is a once-in-a-lifetime opportunity, and that as adults we can fine-tune that realization with a tradition that heightens our gratitude for the world.

We can also learn to see the world as "normal mystics" by seeing it through the eyes of our children. We can find out their worldview by encouraging questions and seeking to see the world in their special way.

Most important, we must never let ourselves, or our children, forget that we are all in God's image. That is the basis for all that follows. If we teach that they are but accidents of chemistry, or very clever animals, we cannot bring them a sense of sanctity and infinite worth. No matter how bad a child may feel, the parent can tell her that if God made her, she must have both a purpose and a capacity to be good and important. To be human is a glorious destiny.

For there to be a sense of "significant being," wrote Heschel, one needs three things: a God, a soul, and a moment. And all three are always present.

QUESTIONS TO DISCUSS
WITH YOUR CHILDREN

1. How do you feel when you see something beautiful in the world?

2. Why do we say blessings? When you say a blessing, does it help you feel God's presence?

3. How does it make you feel to recite a bedtime prayer?

4. What does it mean that you were "created in the image of God"?

5. Why do you believe God made the world?

Origins and Explanations: Where Does God Come from, Did He Write a Book, and Is He a She?

The rabbis relate the following story about Abraham, the first Jew: Abraham's father, Terach, was an idol maker. One night before going to sleep he left young Abraham in charge of the store. When Terach came back in the morning, he saw that the statues were strewn all over the floor, in bits and pieces. He was enraged. "What happened here?" he screamed at Abraham. His son just shrugged and replied: "The idols had a fight." Terach was furious. "They can't fight," he said. "Why, they can't even see or think!" Abraham said calmly, "Then, Father, why do you worship them?"

CHILDREN HAVE ALL sorts of images in their minds about God. Even though God is beyond full human understanding, it falls to adults to offer some images that help children develop their belief in God.

To do that we must deal with some age-old questions: Was God born? What does God look like? Does God have a body? These questions about God's beginnings, and God's nature, are asked from very early on in a child's life.

In time the questions get broader and deeper. Following their functional orientation, children want to know what God *does*. Does God still speak to us the way God is described as speaking to biblical characters? Why or why not?

Sooner or later this brings us to the question of the Bible itself. Who *really* wrote the Bible? Major challenges have been posed to the idea that the Bible is God's own book. There are many levels on which to read this ancient book, and in this chapter we suggest several different ways of understanding it.

In the course of reading the Bible and wondering about God, children begin to realize that they are part of a continuous chain. In each generation, people have struggled to answer the same question: How do we make God real in our lives?

———

"Where did I come from?" Sooner or later every child asks that question. Children are preoccupied with origins. They want to know where they came from and where other things came from. In order to understand the world, children look for beginnings.

That is why one of the most common questions children ask about God is, Where did God come from? And, Does God have parents?

This question is difficult for adults. Our ideas about the origins of God are murky, too. What should we say?

It is helpful to remember how hard it is for *anyone* to understand God. We should not pretend that we have all the answers stored up, ready to go. Sometimes I ask older children the following question: When you were two years old, could you have understood the way you are now? Could you possibly, as a two-year-old, have comprehended what it is to be a twelve-year-old?

Clearly we could not. Now, God is far greater relative to us than we are to a two-year-old. So our understanding of God must be *very* deficient. God is far too grand for us to have anything but a small and partial idea of the Divine. A medieval Jewish philosopher put it this way: "To be great enough to know God, I would have to be God."

When we discuss ideas about God, we base them on three things: on belief, on what we conclude God has communicated to us and to our ancestors, and on our powers of observation and logic. When our children ask questions, we should first make it clear to them that we are seeking to grasp something no human being can fully fathom.

How much we can understand varies with age. When children are very young, their orientation is imaginative and sometimes disconnected. They will not usually pursue a chain of reasoning more than a step or two. Questions about God veer off or involve things that seem unrelated. A simple answer usually suffices.

When the child reaches the early school years, the orientation is functional; that is, they are interested in concrete operations more than abstract questions. They wish to be shown. Ritual objects take on added significance. Speaking of God is at times difficult because there is no picture. Children of early school years are "show me" children. When there is nothing concrete to show, we have to look for other methods.

We can move forward functionally—by speaking of what God *does* rather than who God is. We are better served by concentrating on God's actions rather than God's attributes. "God is the one who made the world" or "God is the one who gave us consciences" is a better approach than "God is the one who is all-powerful."

At all these stages, we should remind ourselves that children tend to be occupied with basic questions. While their parents have moved on to secondary, subtle ideas, children are reexploring the fundamental ones.

So what of God's beginnings? The simple answer is that God has no parents, because unlike everything else in this world, God was not created. God always was. The Bible's most common name for God is a Hebrew term containing all three tenses of the verb "to be"—was, is, and will be. That is how Judaism conceives of God. God has always been, God is, and God will always be.

It is hard to understand things without limits. We cannot really imagine that space has no end or that time always was or that God has no beginning. These are ideas that stretch our imaginations, though we will never grasp them fully.

WHAT DOES GOD LOOK LIKE?

We have explained to our children that God is not like us. God never began, but always was. But this hardly exhausts the questions children pose about God. In thinking about

God, people project themselves upward and wonder if God is like us. So the next logical step is, what does God look like? Does God look like us?

When we first learn about God, some image usually accompanies our belief. The picture of an old man with a beard sitting on a throne in the sky is very tough to uproot from a child's mind. That is partly because of their orientation: concrete images are all they can grasp. As much as frustrated parents may seek to erase or alter that image, it may prove impossible, and attempts to eliminate it may be counterproductive. Belief will change in time. We should not confirm the image—God is *not* an old man in the sky, after all—but we also need not spend too much time and effort worrying about it.

According to the Jewish tradition, God is nonphysical. This does not mean, as Rabbi Harold Kushner points out, that God is "invisible." That word implies that God *has* a body, but we cannot see it. Rather, God is *intangible*—without form. This is a hard enough notion for adults to hang on to. For children it can prove doubly difficult.

One way of explaining this is to draw analogies. Ask your child where love is. You cannot point to love. We point to our hearts, but that is not love. Love, too, is intangible. We feel it, we are sure it is real, it is clearly a force in the world, yet it is not located in any one point. *God, like love, works through people in this world. Love is not the same thing as God, but it is a good way to begin thinking about God.*

That is why we can speak of God's presence. When we say, "God is everywhere," children respond by pointing and asking, "Is God here? Is God in the table? Is God in my drawer?" These sorts of questions show again how hard it is to escape the idea that all things are somehow physical. Feelings may be the best analogy to draw to help the child understand. Love is everywhere, but it is not really in the table or the dresser. Like God, it is intangible.

Love is not a perfect analogy, because feelings are things that originate inside of us. God exists outside of us as well. Nevertheless, love or warmth or caring may be the best way to help children grasp what it means to say that God is real but not tangible.

※ ※ ※

Exercise 1—Exploring Images of God. Try to uncover your children's ideas of God. Are there other important things they cannot see (such as air and sound, as well as love)? Ask them to draw a picture of God or a picture of what God is like. Children can develop some interesting analogies for God. Pictures and descriptions of God should be kept so that as children grow you can see their concepts change.

IS GOD MALE OR FEMALE?

Dear God,
Are boys better than girls? I know you are one, but try to be fair.

Sylvia
(Children's Letters to God)

The problem of God's form does not end with the analogy of love. For we all have a tendency to use our own concepts when speaking of God. In the past half century, people have become aware of how consistently religious traditions tend to refer to God in the male gender. Not only do we refer to "He" in most texts and prayers, but the vast majority of the images, like kingship, tend to reinforce the idea that God is somehow male.

Judaism assumes no such thing. God is intangible and therefore neither male nor female. This is an important beginning. The concept of gender makes no sense when applied to God. It is not that God is "both"—God is neither. To be male or female presumes a body. No matter what exactly goes into making a person a male or a female, neither term makes sense in relation to God.

But theology is one thing, and language is another. Even though we may know that God has no body, it is no accident that children tend to view God as male. A great deal of religious language reinforces that view. So does the popular identification of maleness with authority. In fact, studies have shown that when we try to reorient children's images, even quite young children are often made very uncomfortable. For many children (and adults as well), it is disturbing to speak of God as female or as different in any way from their settled ideas of God.

This problem has many different implications, and there are many schools of thought as to the right approach. Most will not be willing to rewrite classic religious texts: the Hebrew Bible uses mostly the male gender in speaking of God. Some seek to address the problem by being sure to alternate pronouns—to use "She" for God as well as "He." Some seek to avoid pronouns altogether when referring to God, as we have tried to do in this book. (However, when quoting from a source, we reproduce the wording as it stands rather than altering the original.)

Probably most helpful, in the long run, is gradually to teach the child the intangibility of God and make sure that God's many qualities are emphasized. Love, compassion, sternness, majesty, tenderness, watchfulness—these and other attributes are used to describe God by traditional Jewish texts. Such attributes, and not maleness or femaleness—which are not part of God—are the proper descriptive mode.

DOES GOD LOOK LIKE ME?

One thing we should keep in mind is that, even more than their parents, children practice *imitatio hominis*—creating God in their own image. A child who says "God has brown hair like me" should not bring down upon himself a huge theological lecture. We can encourage the child's thoughts, applaud his exploration of God. But we should then ask why he thinks God has brown hair. And we can go on to put in a word to the effect that God, as far as we understand, does not really have hair, clothes, or a face the way we do. God is different from us, without a body.

One might pursue it further, if the child is insistent or upset: It is true that each of us is made in God's image. In that sense, since you have a bit of the Divine spark in you, and you have brown hair, there is a way in which God may be said to have brown hair. But it also means that God is present in people with blond hair, or different-colored skin, or different features. Part of the marvel of God being in human beings is that all human features reflect God (remember the mirror exercise we did in chapter 2). Not only that, but because God has no body there is no "ideal" human being. We are all reflections, images of God. When a child begins to uncover a sense of God in herself, she may be ready to broaden that sense to include God's other creations as well.

GOD AS AN IMAGE OF LIGHT

We know that God cannot be seen. Even though we each bear a bit of God in us, God's essential image can never be seen. So in teaching our children about God, we are telling them that things that *cannot* be seen are the most valuable things in the world. That idea of the importance of what we cannot see can be very hard for children to grasp.

Because of their preoccupation with objects, children tend to be fixed on the visible. Our society caters to this emphasis on the visual. We are saturated with movies, television, billboards, design, fashion—a parade of images. To achieve the "right look" for a person or a product or a production is the focus of enormous energy, talent, and money in modern America.

But Judaism teaches that the greatest reality is precisely the one we *cannot* see. The Talmud teaches that the essence of blessing is in "that which is hidden from the eye." God is more real than a billboard that was built by human beings and will one day be no more. God is more real than all the visible world. To believe is an affirmation of the greatness of the nonmaterial. All human beings live in a world of things.

The religious person also lives in a world beyond things, an intangible world that we approach with our spiritual sense.

Much of our education of children centers on the teaching of the intangible, although we may not often think of it that way. We teach them the importance of ideas. We concentrate on the notion of justice, goodness, mercy. None of these things can be touched. All of them are as important as that which can be seen. To understand the intangibility of God is to take a large step forward in the appreciation of what is truly important.

In other areas of life as children grow, they will come to learn about analogous ideas. They will learn about sound waves. Electricity will be real to them, although they cannot see it. As adults we have to transfer that understanding of the reality of things we cannot see that still profoundly affects our lives.

Light Is a Sign of God. When I speak to children in a sanctuary, I use the example of the eternal light hanging above the ark. Why is light a symbol for God? Because light itself cannot be seen. What we see is not light, but light bouncing off other things—walls, clothes, faces, even particles in the air.

The same is true of God in this world. We cannot see God. God becomes real to us through other things. God becomes real through the beauty of the world, through the actions of people. But God's self, God's essence, remains invisible—or, really, intangible.

Exercise 2—Learning About God Through Light. Sit with your children in a dark room. Put a candle behind you so that they cannot see it. Then light the candle. Ask if they can see the light. They can see that it is light, but they cannot see the light itself. Ask what they can see; the answer is, each other.

Explain how God is like light. Discuss what things we can see in this world because of God's presence. In the end, you may come to the same conclusion—it is through God's presence that we can truly see each other.

———

Just like light, like justice, like goodness, we cannot see God, but we can know God and bring God into this world. I cannot show you goodness, but I can show you an act of goodness. I cannot show you God, but an act of godliness makes God somehow tangible. That is our responsibility in the partnership. We carry the light so that it can be seen.

ARE ALL OUR IMAGES OF GOD GOOD?

Sometimes children's imaginations frighten us. Fairy tales have scary figures and often great brutality. Yet in each generation children are drawn to these tales. We cannot be sure why this is so. Perhaps Bruno Bettelheim's theory is correct, that the tales externalize fears and aggressions that children carry inside themselves. Whatever the reason, we should not expect only sweetness and light in even the healthiest child's imaginings.

So a child's images of God will not always be what we might wish. Studies of children's ideas of God show that they shift, that the same child carries different images at different times. The images have a broad range: there is a friendly God, a loving God, a villainous God. At times God is distant, at other times very close. God is thought of as a king, as a doctor, as a parent (both mother and father), and as many other ideal or feared characters. We should be aware that these and other images will rattle around in a child's head, just as they do for many adults. Still, it is important to remind children that God is not fully like any of these imaginings, and that there is a great gap between the intangible God and all the characters we know on earth.

Although we cannot know what God is, we can at times know what God wants.

DOES GOD STILL SPEAK TO US?

In what way do we know what God wants? One of the most common questions asked by children is why God does not speak to us anymore. God speaks in the Bible. For today's child, the silence is puzzling, even hurtful. "If God still loves us, why doesn't He talk to us?" was the way one third-grader put the question to me. It is one of the many questions that adults ask with the same fervor as their children.

1. *We Have Changed.* One answer to the question is that God never spoke in quite the way we think. In biblical times, ideas about God's speaking were quite different. Peo-

ple heard God in ways that we do not. Perhaps this is because we are more knowing about the world, or perhaps it is that we are less attuned to God's word.

In the biblical book of Samuel, the child Samuel has entered the service of Eli, the high priest. One night God calls to Samuel. Samuel runs to Eli's room and says, "Here I am, you called me!" This scene was repeated three times before Eli finally realized what was happening. He told Samuel that if he should hear the voice again, to say, "Speak, Lord, for Your servant is listening."

Samuel did as Eli told him. When he heard a voice calling his name, Samuel replied, "Speak, Lord, for Your servant is listening" (I Sam. 3:4–10). That was the beginning of God's communication with Samuel.

The story shows how the direction of an older teacher can help a youngster feel the presence of God. Although the call was directed at Samuel, it took the practiced ear of Eli to hear, secondhand, the true origin of the voice. Children who have spiritual longings and experiences may need us to help nudge them to recognize what it is they feel.

And the story of Samuel suggests what we have already said—that there are many different ways to understand God's voice in the world. Different people have different ideas. Some hear the sounds of the world as the voice of Eli, some recognize them as the voice of God. Perhaps the change is not in God, but in us.

Answer: *Different people hear God through different parts of the world. Some hear God in the sounds of nature. Perhaps in ancient times people listened differently.*

2. God Trains Us as a Parent Trains a Child, and Then Lets Go. Another possibility is that God made a decision similar to the decision parents must make. When children are young, parents offer a great deal of direction. They speak clearly and firmly. Children learn about the world and their place in it from their parents' constant correction and guidance.

At a certain point, however, parents must pull back from their children's lives. Now the children know what the parents believe and have to make their own choices. They have graduated from the idea that forbidden conduct will bring their parents' punishment to the idea that they must now make their own choices.

This reflects Jewish teachings as to why God no longer speaks as in biblical times. For the tasks of human beings have been explained. The law has been laid out. The prophets have spoken. The "parent" of the human race has given us guidance. What God envisions as the human mission is essentially understood. The question now is human interpretation and human integrity. We know what we are supposed to do. Whether we will do it or not is our choice.

At a certain point in human history we acquired a basic grounding in right and wrong. There are arguments about ethics, but basic ethical ideas are clear: the responsibility to be good, the evil of injustice, of theft and murder. The question is no longer whether God will tell us what to do, but whether we will listen to what we were told long ago.

So another answer to the child's question is that God no longer speaks because God has left a legacy of teaching for us to study. We can find out what God really wishes to say to us if only we will examine what we have already been told. God may no longer speak, but we may still listen.

Answer: *God has already communicated the most important lessons of life. Now it is up to us to learn them and to live by them.*

Yet another response to this question is that God does speak to us.

3. The Whispering God. In the Bible, in the book of Kings, Chapter 18, the prophet Elijah works a wondrous miracle. It was a time when worshipers of Ba'al, a pagan god, were widespread in Israel. They were encouraged by the queen, Jezebel. So Elijah challenged the priests of Ba'al to a test.

Elijah encouraged them to present a sacrifice to their god, which they did. Despite all their pleading and praying, however, the sacrifice simply lay upon the altar. No god came from heaven to consume it. Hours went by, and nothing happened. Elijah even mocked the priests, telling them to shout louder—maybe their god was asleep or had gone away for a while.

In time, it came to be Elijah's turn to offer a sacrifice. After placing the sacrifice on the altar, he doused it with water. Then Elijah prayed to God, who sent forth a fire from the sky. So intense were the flames that they licked up the water from the sacrifice and consumed the sacrifice itself.

The moment was a triumph for Elijah. After working this wonder, Elijah, we might suppose, was safe and revered as a prophet. Instead his life was threatened by Queen Jezebel. He ran to the wilderness. There, depressed and forlorn, he wished to die. Elijah had expected that once Israel beheld the miracle, the people would return to God and to God's prophets. Instead he became a hunted man. It seemed nothing he could do, no matter how spectacular, would persuade this nation to return to God.

In the midst of his depression, an angel appeared to Elijah and heartened him. Encouraged and revived with the help of this angel, Elijah wandered until he arrived at the top of the mount of Horeb. There, the Bible tells us, there was a mighty wind that split mountains, but God was not in the wind. There was an earthquake, but God was not in the earthquake. Then there was a fire, but God was not in the fire. This was followed by a *kol d'mama daka,* a still, small voice (or, in another translation, a thin voice of silence). In that voice, God asks Elijah why he is out in the wilderness and tells him to return to the people.

Why does God send various natural marvels but wait to speak until the *kol d'mama daka?* It overturns our expectations. We expect God's voice to be thunderous. Elijah, God seems to be saying, you expect impressive miracles. You want me to appear like fire from the sky. But God does not really work that way in people's lives. God touches the heart softly.

When we teach our children about God's word, we should teach them that it is not the fire out of the sky, but the slow change of heart; not the night vision of angels flying, but the vision of a spirit awakening, of a person's gradual maturity and sensitivity blossoming. God speaks inside us, but we must often be still, even silent, to hear.

Does God still speak to us? Yes, although not perhaps in the thunderous voice reported in some parts of the Bible. God speaks in tones of conscience and duty, of compassion and goodness. We want our children to be able to hear those internal voices. It is not that God is silent, but soft-spoken. Whatever may have happened in the past, the God of our day is a whispering God. God demands that we be good listeners.

Answer: *God does speak to us. Sometimes we have to be very quiet inside to hear.*

※ ※ ※

Exercise 3—Have You Heard God's Voice? Sometimes we understand what we do only in retrospect. Together with your children, make a life tree: straight where your life remained the same for a while; branches where you took a slightly different direction for a brief time; the trunk (or main path if you use the symbol of a road map) veering off where your life changed a lot—when you moved, went to a new school, and so on.

Then look at the key moments of change. Do you believe God was in any of those moments? We could each do many things at decisive moments of our lives. Ask your children if in their key moments they were whispered to, or nudged, by God.

WHO WROTE THE BIBLE?

One of the ways people have for centuries sought to hear the voice of God is through the texts of tradition. Again and again in talking about God, we return to the Bible. In Judaism, study is a very important value. In learning, in stories, in study, we discover much of what God wishes to teach. We also learn a lot about what we have inside ourselves. But we need to form a clearer idea of what it is we are studying and why.

Discussing who wrote the Bible is one of the touchiest subjects in religious life. Passions flare when the issue is even approached. Yet we cannot avoid it. In returning to sacred texts together with our children, we have to puzzle over what makes them sacred.

Discussions about who wrote the Bible begin to take place in preadolescence. Usually, for younger children, to call a book holy is sufficient. Once the question is raised at any age, however, it deserves to be taken seriously.

Traditional Jewish belief holds that the Torah* was dictated to Moses at Sinai. With some variations, that belief held for many generations.

In time, several things disrupted that belief. One was the idea that the Bible taught things that science contradicted, such as the claim that the world was created in seven days. Even more difficult, books from other cultures were found that contained material similar (at times even identical) to the Bible and were written earlier. It began to appear that the Bible had been written by human beings who used the same idioms and ideas as many of their contemporaries.

Our children will hear of all these challenges to the Bible. What follows are three major challenges and some re-

---

* Sometimes the word *Torah* refers to the whole body of Jewish sacred writings. The Torah here refers to the five books of Moses: Genesis, Exodus, Leviticus, Numbers, and Deuteronomy. The Bible refers to the whole corpus of biblical literature, which includes many other books. Traditionally Judaism has a tripartite division: the Torah, the Prophets, and the Writings, (called in Hebrew *Tanach*). Books of history such as Samuel and Kings are included along with Isaiah, Jeremiah, and so on among the prophetic books, while Psalms, Proverbs, and various other works are included among the Writings.

sponses that you can discuss with your children when the questions arise.

Science as a Challenge to the Bible. The challenge of science is not as serious as it may appear. Very early on in Jewish history, some commentators recognized that the Torah was not a scientific textbook. Its intention was to talk not so much about the duration of creation as about its meaning. One can easily read the Bible with absolute confidence as to its Divine origin and still understand that accounts such as that of creation are not meant to give specific details of the scientific origins of the universe. It teaches us the purpose of creation and the Author of creation. The Torah is a guide for life, not a biology textbook or an archaeological survey.

Science is engaged in teaching the how, and the Torah teaches the why. Science will not tell us why to get up in the morning, why to be good, why life has meaning. Indeed, quite the opposite. I recall learning in biology class that the chemicals that make up our bodies would sell for a few dollars in the chemist's shop. It is the Torah that tells us that the combination of ingredients, when they come together to form a person, is beyond price.

To know how God made the world, through what evolutionary processes or physical marvels, is not the province of a religious education. It is not the task of the Torah.

Response: *Science and the Bible teach us different things. Science teaches us how the world works. Our faith teaches us how to act, what is important, and what to hope for.*

The Challenge of Other Civilizations. The second challenge to the Bible is that of comparative study with other texts and civilizations. Many find it hard to believe the Torah is divine when it contains stories or ideas identical to those of other, contemporaneous civilizations. Ideas that were considered divine have their origins in older societies.

Defenders of the divinity of the Torah make the argument that God was communicating in terms that would be understood by ancient Israelites. They knew certain ideas and terms, so God simply took those ideas, changed them, added to them, and refined them. After all, God *could* have dictated the U.S. Constitution, but it would have done little good for ancient Israelites, for whom such notions would have been incomprehensible. God spoke the language of the time, even when it repeated what others were saying.

Response: *God speaks to people in whatever language they can understand.*

Moral Challenges to the Bible. Last, some dismiss the divinity of the Bible because parts of it are morally objectionable. It is hard to read of God ordering the Israelites to fight bloody wars. It is hard to see that the Bible permits slavery, however much we recognize that slavery in the Bible is far more humane than it has been in other societies. It has been argued that God was seeking to end these practices but could not do so all at once. Israel had to be gradually weaned away from customs that were common in the ancient world.

Some will simply say that God's purposes are not always understood. That is true, but it can also be a justification for very bad behavior. Perhaps the best answer we can give is that God must work through people in this world, and people themselves are often cruel.

Most of the immorality in the Bible comes from the

people themselves. Indeed, the Bible argues for its own accuracy by being so honest. Flaws are not hidden, even in the greatest heroes. When biblical heroes commit terrible sins, like murder or adultery, the Bible does not gloss over the facts. Israel is portrayed not as perfect, but as a sometimes weak and foolish people who have moments of greatness and moments of pettiness. What other nation willingly records its origins as an enslaved and despised people? Before we reject the truthfulness of the Bible, we have to ask ourselves: Why would an individual, or a people, make up such stories about himself? Perhaps we can see the hand of God in the sometimes brutal honesty the Bible brings to its subjects.

The Bible rises above the ancient world, but it is also a part of it. It makes sense that God would choose a backward and small people to bring a message to the world. Had God chosen a powerful and perfect people, their own abilities would have been the reason given for their success. The immorality of Israel is in a way a proof that these people could not alone have brought the message of God to the world. God must have had a hand in allowing a tiny, wandering tribe to change the world.

Response: *Sometimes people, including our ancestors, do terrible things. But we can learn from their mistakes as well as their good deeds.*

However we answer these difficult and complicated issues, they must be dealt with when we speak to our children. We do them no service in pretending that moral questions and conflicts do not exist. They will certainly discover them for themselves one day.

THE BIBLE'S INFLUENCE

Despite the moral predicaments the Bible poses, we cannot lightly dismiss its triumphs. The question of where the Bible came from is important, but even more important is the question of its impact on history. No matter where it came from, the Bible's effect commands respect and attention. Generations have seen it as a book of profound wisdom and depth.

The story is told of a tour guide in the Louvre who is showing the Mona Lisa to a group of tourists. One of them says, "Well, I don't see what is so great about this painting. It seems pretty ordinary to me!" To which the guide answers, "Sir, we no longer judge the Mona Lisa. Now, the Mona Lisa judges us." The same may be said of the Bible. Clearly it is an extraordinary book; history has long since pronounced its verdict.

That this book, among the billions written in history, should have survived so long, that it spawned two other great religions (Christianity and Islam), marks it as something not so easily explained. In addition to its influence in the past, the Bible retains its power today. Until recently, Jews would try to smuggle Bibles into the Soviet Union for other Jews to read, because the book was banned. For a world superpower to fear a three-thousand-year-old book in an age of satellites and rocket ships reminds us of the Bible's remarkable power.

The first verse of the Bible I ever learned was God's initial command to Abraham (Gen. 12:1): *"Lech lecha"*— "Go forth." Our teacher explained that the Hebrew could mean both go out from your home into the world, and go

into yourself. God was teaching Abraham that journeying through the world would teach him about himself, and
that journeying into himself would bring him, eventually,
to God.

Suddenly, as a child, my eyes were opened to the possibility of a book where words held many meanings. I learned
about a book to which I could return over and over and
discover more about God, the world, and myself. I did not
think about who wrote down Abraham's story. All I knew
was that I wanted to travel along with him.

HOW DO WE DESCRIBE THE BIBLE TO OUR CHILDREN?

The experience of many readers is that the Bible has a quality that is different from great literature. The difference is
not the quality of the writing. Parts of the Bible are very
artistic and other parts less so. Throughout the book, however, a sense of the deepest issues of life runs through each
character and scene. Human struggle and divine counsel are
so real on the pages that they move us beyond the merit of
the writing or the details of the story.

Could human beings have brought their own ideas and
interpretations to this book? Perhaps it is the product of an
encounter with God, the story that was told by a people
who had a direct, powerful experience of God at the beginning of history. Perhaps certain messages and ideas that God
offered to humanity were given shape by people. Maybe that
is why the Bible tells so many different types of stories. With
both divinity and humanity in it, the Bible speaks to us

eternally and yet invites our own encounter with the story or our own evaluation of its message.

How shall we describe the Bible to our children?

1. *The Diary of a People.* A colleague, Dr. Daniel Gordis, once offered the following analogy: Pretend that one day you were wandering through the house that your great-great-grandparents had lived in generations before. Walking in the attic, you stepped on a loose floorboard. After prying it off, you uncovered the diary of your great-great-grandmother.

Imagine with what care and interest you would read that book! You would scrutinize its pages again and again. It told you where you came from and who you are. In it you would read so much about what shaped you. Many of the patterns of life recorded in the diary might recur in your own life.

That is what the Bible is for the Jewish people. It is our family diary, preserved for thousands of years. It tells us where we came from and suggests our destination. The Jews are a tiny people, less than 3 percent of the population of America and less than 1 percent of that of the world. How have we managed to survive when so many others have disappeared? The family diary helps us to understand.

The themes of the Bible, of exile and difficulty, of moral achievement, of family dynamics, of the search for God, recur often in Jewish history. "The deeds of the ancestors foreshadow the lives of the children" is an old Jewish principle found in reading the Bible. The family diary tells us what our own lives mean. It is the foundation document of the Jewish people.

Description: *The Bible is the family story of our people. We read it to know where we came from and to help us understand where we are going.*

2. As a World Classic. The Bible is also the foundation document of Western civilization. To read the Bible with a child is not only to teach her her people's history. It is to acquaint her with the central stories of Western culture, the stories without which so much else remains unknown and unclear.

To read the Bible is to get a profound cultural education in one book. The central shaping ideas of Western civilization are taken from its pages.

Description: *The Bible is so rich that many great writers and artists took their ideas from it. To understand their great works, we need to understand the book they thought was so important.*

3. As a Moral Guide. The Bible is a book of instruction on how to live. Each day our age produces a new classic on how to live. The bookshelves in stores are jammed with advice on being happy. Fresh philosophies crowd the shelves. Which theory should parents advance to their children? What should we do when the latest theorist, whose face is on all the talk shows and whose book is on all the best-seller lists, is pushed aside tomorrow by a newer idea? Where do we turn for guidance that is not fashionable but fixed—something that will last?

We need more than a reliable source to help us ensure our child's physical health. We need a guide to moral health as well. Which expert should we rely upon to train our children's souls?

For generations parents and educators have turned to the Bible and to the traditions that grow out of the Bible. They are there to help us grow in soul.

When we read these Bible stories, we recall that however much has changed, one thing remains: human nature. We still fight and cry and love, as did our ancestors. The Bible grants us a true window into the human heart.

Description: *The Bible teaches us how to live. We learn from the struggles of Moses and David, of Rebecca and Ruth.*

4. As a Dialogue of Lovers. The central character in the Bible is God. Part of the Bible's emotional power is that since God grants human beings the chance to do what they want, God is often frustrated, angry, even seemingly hurt. To read the Bible carefully is to see how God and human beings search for each other in this world. There are elements of submission, rebellion, misunderstanding—and love.

Among the many names God bears in the Jewish tradition is that of *El Emunah*—the God of Faith. One rabbinic comment explains that this means that God has faith, too—faith in humanity. The Bible records the testing and, eventually, the strengthening of this faith. In its way it is as tumultuous and passionate a love story as can be found anywhere. It is a drama, a romance, and a story of beginnings in each generation.

Description: *Just as people write love letters to one another, the Bible talks about the love between us and God. We read it to understand the meaning of that love.*

Finally, two ways to read the Bible that require no description for our children but are very important:

5. *As a Story.* The Bible contains some wonderful stories. They are gripping, filled with passion and drama. Among its many other virtues, the Bible can be read as a book that tells us the kinds of stories that stay with us throughout our lives.

6. *As a Treasury of Heroes.* One of the sad parts of growing up in modern America is that we have few worthy heroes. Children watch movies that make heroes out of killers and con men. They watch sports events and adore athletes, many of whom are wonderfully skilled but are surely not the sort of people we hope our children will grow up to be. Where do we find true heroes, the kind who will influence our children for good?

The Bible contains such heroes. When they make mistakes, the Bible does not hesitate to criticize. But they are striving for something worthy. Ruth or Jonathan will be healthier for any child to admire than this week's movie sensation. The Bible can help us shape our children's ideas about what is worth imitating.

For all these reasons and more, the Bible has proved invaluable throughout the ages. It speaks to us as parents, as teachers, as readers, as seekers. It will speak to our children as well if we give it the chance.

Exercise 4—A Story Before Bedtime. Once a week, instead of the usual story you read to your child, try a Bible tale. It might be taken straight out of the Bible or from one of the many children's Bibles available. Read the story beforehand and determine the appropriate age level.

Either that night or the next day, bring up the story again. Find out how the child felt about the heroes, about the ideas, about God's place in the story. Childhood stories live in a deep place inside us; reading from the Bible once a week can provide stories that will grow with your child.

ARE THERE RELIGIOUS TALES BEYOND THE BIBLE?

The Bible's richness has resulted in a vast amount of commentary. For thousands of years interpretations and legends have explained and expanded on the biblical text. This material too is often inspiring and beautiful—and much of it is written especially for children.

The Bible tends to be very sparing of words. Unlike other literature, it leaves much of its message unsaid. The difference is almost like the difference between listening to a drama on radio or watching it on television. On television nothing is left to the imagination. All the characters have faces, all the details are in the picture, and we watch passively, receiving the images.

Listening to the radio, one is forced to picture what

people look like, what the world looks like. We participate in creating the action. Reading the Bible is like that. Dialogue is usually brief and to the point. Description of people's appearance is rare. We do not know from the Bible, for example, if Moses was tall or short, bearded or smooth-shaven, fat or thin. The reader is invited to plunge in and imagine how these things really were.

So the Bible invites us and our children to exercise our imaginations. And because others have done the same for generations, we can read endless tales that supplement the Bible.

The collection of legends is called the Midrash. They were written by rabbis, most of whom lived in Israel in the first few centuries of the common era. The story at the outset of this chapter about Abraham smashing his father's idols is from the Midrash. These tales, fantasies, and interpretations help us understand our religious roots and aid us in our own spiritual search.

NOT "DOES GOD EXIST?" BUT "IS GOD REAL?"

In this chapter, we have tried to address two different sorts of questions: What is God like? and How does God communicate with us? Both questions should lead us to action. One thing Judaism has always insisted upon: No matter how abstract the question, it has to be brought into the world; it has to have some meaning for how we live now. In this sense Judaism shares the functional orientation of children. God must make a difference.

For many of us, the question is not whether God exists. The question is whether God makes a difference, whether God is real in our lives. For a number of years I have taught classes in Jewish theology to college students, both Jewish and non-Jewish. I have presented the traditional philosophical proofs for God—the ontological proof, the cosmological proof, the teleological proof. I diagram each one on the board and explain it to the students.

Never once in my class have I seen a student study these arguments, clap his or her forehead, and exclaim, "Aha! Now I believe!" For belief is more than an intellectual process. When we answer the questions of children, or of seekers of any age, we are answering their hearts as well as their minds. We are making demands on their behavior. You cannot believe in God, be honest with yourself, and not have it change the way you live your life.

That is why it is important to figure out how to look for God. Seeking God is not just an intellectual search. The intellect is an important part of the search, but the search itself is much broader. Rather, it is about how we teach ourselves and our children to look at life. How do we make God not just "true," but real?

QUESTIONS TO DISCUSS
WITH YOUR CHILDREN

1. Do you picture God? If so, what do you imagine God looks like?

2. Do you think God is male or female?

3. What other images do you have of God? What is God like? (Is God like a king, a parent, a police officer, a friend, a schoolteacher?)

4. What would you most like to understand about God?

5. Does God talk to you? Why or why not?

6. Who do you believe wrote the Bible?

7. Apart from God, what are important things in the world that we cannot see?

4

Hide-and-Seek:
Where to Look for God

A Chasidic story: A little child's father found him cowering behind a bush, crying. "Why are you crying?" he asked. "Because," said his son, "we were playing hide-and-seek, and no one came to look for me."

His father looked sad. "You know," he told his son, "God makes the same complaint of human beings. God hides from us, and we do not care enough to search."

WHERE DO WE teach our children to look for God? There are many places to find God in the world. We can search for God in the origins of things, at births and beginnings. We can search for God in the beauty of the world.

One of the most important places to look for God is in one another. Since we are the image of God, each person is a reflection of the Divine. God is also found in sacred moments, when we gather together to celebrate or even to grieve.

God is found in the family. In the Bible, God begins

with families and builds to community. For God is also present in community, in the way we share with those beyond our own homes. Building a community is bringing God's presence into the world.

Finally, we must teach our children that God is found inside ourselves. The reason there are so many places to find God in the world is not only that the world is so charged with God, but that we bring God to the world. Our own souls are the starting point.

———

LOOKING FOR GOD IN ORIGINS

God is in beginnings. We might say that God is inside the first ring of the tree—the force that brings things into being. The Bible opens with creation. That opening reminds us where God is to be found, at dawn and birth and beginnings.

Many people experience a sense of God that is entirely new to them at the birth of a child. It is as if the instant of creation is being repeated. Somehow God is closer at the inception of life. When we speak of the miracle of new life, we are noticing the miracle of beginnings.

One of the characteristics of Judaism is to take the cycle of life, things that recur each year like the new season, and see them as fresh starts. We mentioned before that many experiences are marked with the blessing "Blessed are You, Lord our God, King of the Universe, Who has kept us in life, sustained us, and enabled us to reach this day." That blessing is said when we taste the first fruit of the new season, and we invoke God not only when something is entirely new, but when something long gone returns. God is recalled when we greet the spring, the new fruit, even when we take out seasonal clothing long stored away. After enough time, every return is also a beginning. We see old things anew. The first peach of the year tastes different from the last peach of the previous year. That magic return reminds us of God. Each cycle is a new beginning.

In children, origins are a powerful preoccupation. When children ask where they came from, we owe them not just a scientific tale, but a spiritual saga. We come from God. Our origin is in eternity, to which we return. No one truly has humble beginnings.

▨ ▨ ▨

Exercise 1—Seeing the Origins of Life. To see the birth of an animal is a powerful experience for a child. It can be your own pet cat or dog. You may be lucky enough to see a birth at the local zoo or on a farm. To be able to recite the blessing above at the birth of one of God's creations is a moving experience.

The sprouting of new plants and new leaves offers a similar opportunity. The old standby of placing a seed in soil inside a styrene cup still works its magic. Watching one living thing spring from another reminds us of God, who is at the beginning of all life. The natural world is always ending and beginning, a lesson for life and a path to God.

———

God is also found at the beginning of certain life stages. At a Bar or Bat Mitzvah, for example, the same blessing (called in Hebrew the *Shehechiyanu*) is recited. It marks the onset of a new phase of life. At an earlier stage, a baby's first words and first steps are times when we may see the shaping hand of God in our daily lives, when things begin.

LOOKING FOR GOD IN BEAUTY

When we discussed the idea of normal mysticism, we mentioned that God can be found in the natural world. When we see sunsets, horizons, oceans, and mountains, all this beautiful array of our world can bring us closer to God.

The experience of beauty touches us deep inside. Different landscapes will appeal to different tastes. As parents we can try to arrange our children's world so that they have the chance to see the magnificence of the created world. Children should not believe that the whole world is pavement and streetlights.

When I was a teenager, I took a bus across country. I left from Philadelphia and arrived in Los Angeles four days and three nights later. At the time, I was quite confirmed in my atheism. Thoughts of God did not often cross my mind.

On the third day, the bus drove through the Colorado Rockies. I remember looking out the window and feeling as though nothing but the deliberate sculpting of a divine hand could possibly have fashioned something so grand. It did not change my mind about God. I arrived in Los Angeles with the same disbelief with which I had left Philadelphia. But the moment stayed with me. It gave me a glimpse into a side of the world that was not simply beauty, but something above beauty, a sense that the world was charged with grandeur. Now I see that sense as a moment of God's reaching toward me and of finding a sense of God in myself. I was not ready to recognize it as such, but God, like any good parent, is patient.

LOOKING FOR GOD INSIDE OTHER INDIVIDUALS

There is a Jewish mystical belief that sparks of God are scattered throughout creation. Our task as human beings is to recognize and raise those sparks. By raising the sparks we aid in the redemption of the world.

The most important sparks are those inside each of us. For many who seek God, the search has to start inside ourselves. How do we understand looking for God inside ourselves?

Judaism trains people to see each other in a special way. Deep faith does not see people only as they are; it sees people as what they have the potential to be. Faith teaches us to look inside for our possibilities. From our earliest moments God is within us, and so we are capable of great things.

Judaism is concerned at all times with bringing people to a higher plane. That means we should not limit ourselves and others or think we have exhausted everything inside us. We violate the intent of Judaism when we shut down our spirit.

We tend to use the word *potential* with children. To be a child is to have potential. How many times do we call in children who have done something wrong, or failed at some task through lack of effort, and exclaim, "You have such potential!" Of course, adults have potential, too. No one loses their potential at age thirty, or fifty, or ninety. There is always more in us, more that is untapped. We never exhaust all we are. We cannot deplete all of our powers because we have within a spark of God, which is limitless.

Stories of unsuspected potential in human beings abound. Perhaps the greatest philosopher of modernity, Immanuel Kant, is famous for books he began to write at age fifty-seven. Grandma Moses began to paint in her eighties. In the Jewish tradition, Rabbi Akiva, the most renowned of the rabbinic sages, did not even know the Hebrew alphabet until he began to study at age forty. Potential lurks inside each of us. There is always more, because it is more than a trick of genetic inheritance, it is a spiritual endowment.

When we see possibilities in our children, it is not only a testament to their youth. To see potential is a testament to their humanity. At every age we should see possibility, even when we are at first discouraged.

The Maggid of Dubnov, a renowned Jewish storyteller, once told the following tale. A king was in possession of a beautiful diamond, which he cherished. Each night he would take it out and look at it and marvel at his good fortune. One night the diamond slipped from his hands and fell with a sharp snap on the floor. When the king picked it up he saw, to his dismay, that a thin crack now ran through the length of the diamond.

The king was frantic. He called upon all the expert

craftsmen of the realm, but they were unanimous: once a crack has developed in a diamond, it cannot be restored.

In desperation the king sent word throughout the kingdom that anyone able to repair his diamond would be generously rewarded. In time an old man, a jeweler from a far province, appeared. He promised to fix the king's diamond.

Months went by, and the appointed day arrived. There was great anxiety in the court. Everyone was terrified lest the king be disappointed. Then there was no knowing what he might do.

The jeweler walked into the palace and presented a box to the king. The king opened it slowly and looked at his diamond. His face reddened in anger—the crack still ran down the center of his precious stone.

The king began to shout, but the jeweler cut him off: "Your Majesty, turn the jewel over." When the king turned it over, he saw that the jeweler had carved the petals of a blossom at the very top of the diamond. The line running through it was no longer a crack, it was now the stem of a flower, and the stone was more beautiful than ever.

That is what it means to see potential. We recognize that human frailties are not merely cracks. They can be turned to beauty. When children understand that flaws can be carved into flowers, they are stepping closer to appreciating themselves and relating to God.

SEEING PROMISE IN THOSE
WHO ARE CLOSE

A marvelous story is told in the Bible of Samuel's anointing of the new king. God has decided to depose the previous king, Saul, and sends the high priest Samuel to find a new king. God sends Samuel to the house of one Jesse the Bethlehemite. Samuel is told that there, among Jesse's sons, the new king will be found.

Samuel dutifully goes off to Jesse's house and asks him to present his sons. Jesse brings out his firstborn son, Eliab. He is a tall, handsome, strapping figure of man. Samuel thinks to himself that this must be God's new king.

At that point God speaks to Samuel. God tells Samuel that Eliab has been rejected. Why? Because not as people see does God see. "For man sees only what is visible, but the Lord sees into the heart" (1 Sam. 16:7).

Jesse then calls all seven of his sons, and none of them is the new king. The search seems to have failed.

Finally Samuel asks Jesse, "Are you certain these are all your boys?" Jesse suddenly remembers the little one, who is out back tending the sheep. Samuel tells him to bring in this child. So Jesse sends for his youngest, and in comes the boy, young, bright-eyed, and ruddy-cheeked. God tells Samuel to rise and anoint this child, for he is David, the new king of Israel.

What is startling about that story is that Jesse not only assumed David would not be king—he forgot even to introduce him! Like the child who sits quietly in his room upstairs, David was not even presented to the company.

David's remarkable qualities lay hidden even from his own father.

Every teacher has had this experience. A little girl sits at the back of the class and rarely if ever speaks. The teacher disregards her. One day, as if out of nowhere, the child says or does something remarkable. We have learned again the lesson of human potential.

For Judaism, this is not just a reminder of ability; it is a statement of spirit. To see people as repositories of the Divine is an act of faith. To teach our children that people are creations of God is to remind them that there is no exhausting the possibilities inside another human being. There is always more, there is always untapped capacity.

Sometimes it is very hard to believe in the specialness of those we know well. To see strangers as magical is easy. They are far away, and distance blurs flaws. The poet Dante idealized Beatrice, the woman who in his *Divine Comedy* leads Dante through Heaven. That idealization hides the fact that Dante did not really know Beatrice, hardly ever spoke to her, that he fell in love from afar. She was perfect because they did not touch. We can all exalt stars we see through telescopes. The trick is to love the earth underfoot.

Each Friday night at the dinner table there is a blessing that a parent intones over each child. For male children it is "May you be like Ephraim and Menasseh," for female children "May you be like Sarah, Rebecca, Rachel, and Leah." Both are then followed by the threefold, priestly blessing "May God bless you and keep you. May God cause His countenance to shine upon you and be gracious to you. May God turn His countenance to you and grant you peace."

The blessing is a way of connecting and of affirming love

at a critical moment. But there is more to that blessing. By wishing that the male son be like biblical characters (who combine both learning and worldly accomplishment) and that female children become like the biblical matriarchs, the parent is hoping for the ideal in the child. We are seeing potential, the spark of divinity, in what is close. Even more important, each child knows that he or she is loved, the focus of dreams.

Children should be brought to understand that people are bearers of the Divine in this special way. Limitations we put on people based on background or history must always be tentative and subject to change. God lurks in unlikely places and unlikely people. The most remarkable plants grow out of unpromising soil.

WHAT IS AN I – THOU ENCOUNTER?

The Jewish philosopher Martin Buber developed what he called a "dialogic" philosophy. His observation was that most of the time we relate toward others for a specific end. When we deal with people, we usually have some goal in mind. We are aiming toward some benefit from the relationship.

The problem with that, as Buber noted, is then we relate only to the part of the person that can help us achieve our goal. If I want you to get me a glass of water, I am relating only to that part of you that is capable of providing me with water. I am treating you as a means—the means of providing me with water—rather than an end in yourself. So we treat people as tools to accomplish things for us, rather than as full human beings.

Even when we relate to people in emotional ways, we may be treating them as means. If I call you to complain, I am relating only to the part of you that will listen to me and sympathize. I am not really concerned with all of you, just with the piece that can help me. Buber called such relationships "I–It" relationships. We are using another person. We want them to be a particular way, for our benefit.

Such meetings are not full experiences. Since we are relating only to a part of another person, we bring only a part of ourselves as well. In such encounters we are often thinking of something else. Our mind wanders, and we are paying only partial attention. We talk to someone, but we are really thinking about where we have to be next, what we will have for dinner, or how we can gracefully end the conversation. It is a conversational equivalent of shaking hands—only two small parts of each person are really touching.

Now there is nothing really wrong with these sorts of encounters, said Buber. People do, after all, need glasses of water and shoulders to cry on. You cannot always give all of yourself. Yet indispensable as those encounters are, we all feel that there must be more. In Buber's own words, "Man cannot live without the realm of 'it.' But one who lives with 'it' alone is not a man." There are also times when we must relate to the full person. This encounter Buber calls I–Thou.

At times, Buber says, we have moments when we encounter other people in all their being. We do not want anything from them. We are not distracted by other thoughts when we are talking to them. We are fully present, truly giving of ourselves, and experiencing the other person.

Such an I–Thou encounter may be very brief. It may

lapse and then be renewed. Close friends, parents and children, husbands and wives may find their lives made up of thousands of such moments, along with all the everyday, mundane moments of life. The key is that we do have flashes when we see another human being, when we look into their eyes, and two souls open to each other.

When that happens, Buber says, we are not only seeing another person, we are glancing at the face of God. "In every particular thou is a glimpse of the Eternal Thou," says Buber. In other words, since a person has within a spark of God, when we fully encounter a person, we catch a glimpse of God. We come to understand the Divine when we are more receptive to human beings.

Children, too, are accustomed to treating people as means. Every child, after all, needs certain things from his parents. But the relationship of need is not everything. Because children need so much, they may assume that need is all the parent–child relationship is built on. The parent's job is to teach that need is not a foundation, that need is the outgrowth of underlying love.

There are moments when parents and children see each other in their fullness. These moments of love are shot through with sacredness. We can ourselves learn, and teach our children, that to see another truly is to see something of God.

Sometimes we are inclined to let those magical instants pass. Perhaps we are embarrassed, or we do not know how to handle those moments. The magic is that nothing need be *done* with them. They simply are—and in experiencing them together with our children, we are forever enriching our relationships.

There are times when we need to stop stepping back.

Parents spend a great deal of energy discussing their children. Adults analyze kids, evaluate them, test them, worry over them. Important as that is, analysis alone does not relate to the whole child. Following Buber's counsel, there are times simply to experience them.

A story is told of three astronauts who went into space. Upon returning, they were asked what they thought of the experience. One said, "I kept thinking, the world looks so small from outer space—the universe is so vast." The second answered, "I was astonished to think how much had happened on that globe that I could see. All the wars, the loves, the dramas, all on that small orb." The third astronaut shrugged and said, "You know, all I could think was—why didn't I bring a camera!"

Sometimes as parents we are so busy measuring, recording, and analyzing that we forget to experience. Unwittingly we teach our children that if something hasn't been caught by the videocamera, it doesn't matter. But moments live in life, not in pictures. Children and parents should have moments. Let them find God in each other. In their way, such instants outlast even pictures and videotapes. Because moments when we see God in others help shape our lives. I–Thou relationships change us and deepen our gratitude for the marvel of God's world.

❊ ❊ ❊

Exercise 2—Being Open to I–Thou Encounters with Your Child. The key to this exercise is that it is not really an exercise. There is nothing to *do*. Instead it asks you to be receptive to those moments when your contact with your child reaches deep connection. You cannot force a moment of deep intimacy, but you can be open to it and value it when it comes along. You can allow yourself to feel how such moments are made up of holiness as well as of love.

The next step is to try to express your sense of holiness and love to your children, so that they will become accustomed to seeing sanctity in such encounters in their own lives.

LOOKING FOR GOD
IN SACRED MOMENTS

Judaism tries to provide openings for just such sacred encounters. In ritual moments there is an opportunity for togetherness where people can reach toward each other and reach toward God.

It is not surprising that studies show that the more ritually observant the family, the lower the incidence of divorce. Part of that is no doubt due to the social orthodoxy of certain families. The more traditional the family unit, the more traditional the community, the more divorce is likely to be discouraged. But there is another factor, at least equally important, that I can attest to from my own experience.

In my parents' house we always had Friday night (Sabbath) dinner together. We could not go to the movies or see a game. We did not watch television or listen to the radio during the meal. In other words, we were forced to talk to each other.

I say "forced" because even though these were some of

the most wonderful moments of my childhood, given the option, I would probably have watched television instead. That is simply human nature. Given a choice of sitting around the television or sitting around talking, how many families willingly choose the latter? It is harder. It is also more rewarding.

Jewish ritual aims at regular behavior. Traditionally, Sabbath candles are lit every Friday night. Although in some homes this is done sporadically, the intent of the tradition is constancy. That is because Judaism understands that if given a choice, we will often choose the way that is easier but less enriching.

The ritual forced our family to be together, to get to know one another, to laugh and argue and encounter. We had chances to be drawn close. The ritual pressed our souls together.

Dr. Alvin Mars, director of the Brandeis-Bardin Institute, once told me that when he and his wife, Marilyn, first got married, they dreamed of Sabbath dinners when the family would sit around and talk and enjoy one another. The atmosphere would be warm and loving and the conversation filled with interest and laughter.

Then they had kids.

What happened? The children made noise and wanted to leave and were bored—they were real kids, not fantasies. And it is pretty rare for real live adolescents to name sitting around a family dinner table as their first choice of activity.

However, said Alvin, now that his children are grown, what do they say to him? "Gee, Dad, remember those great Sabbath dinners we used to have together? Weren't they the best?" The force of ritual stays with us, reminding us of sacred moments as well as family closeness, and through that family closeness, we are drawn closer to God.

Ritual creates a sacred atmosphere. Many people feel uneasy because they are not quite sure how to do it. A number of books and teachers can help (see further reading suggestions on page 234). It is understandable that ritual is awkward for those who grew up without it. It takes time.

But the remarkable thing is that the magic works. Often we feel that we cannot create this sacred atmosphere because we ourselves are insecure or uncertain of how we feel or unknowledgeable about religious practice. This is where it is important to put your trust in the tradition. It really does work, which is one reason why it has lasted so long.

A family can begin with simple acts. Take the Sabbath meal, for example. The lighting of candles, the presence of challah and wine, even a blessing before, can change the feel of the home. Suddenly it is sacred space.

One way to think of ritual is as another way of speaking to each other. Ritual is a language of symbols and gestures. We all know there are certain gestures that are more powerful than words, that express things words cannot fully express. Raise a flag to half-staff, and you have touched something deeper than words. Put your arms around someone in a moment of sorrow, and the gesture itself is so powerful that nothing needs to be said.

That is how ritual works as well. It is a language we speak to each other, and to God. Unlike words, however, two people can "speak" the ritual at the same time to each other, and both will be understood. It is something each does for himself and both do together.

There are many ways to communicate with God. We

choose ritual because it is time tested, a language that has been used for thousands of years and is used by millions in the world today. In other words, we choose it for the same reasons we choose to speak English.

We could invent another language to speak to one another. But that takes time, and others would not share our language. More important is that we could not possibly in our lifetime invent a language as rich as English. People have been speaking English for a long time, and many generations have contributed their insights, their life experience, and their words to the language. We draw on all of that when we speak it.

The same is true of ritual. Each person can develop his or her own method for speaking to God, but it will not be as fruitful as the tradition, which spans so many lives, lands, and years. Why should we speak to God in an impoverished language? Ritual is rich in meaning; it helps us keep in touch.

That God wishes to be in dialogue with us is the basis of ritual behavior. A woman once anxiously told me that she used to be ritually observant, but over time her observance slipped away. It made her sad and worried. She wondered if God loved her less. I told her that I did not believe that God loved her less, but I did believe that God missed her.

Abraham Joshua Heschel once wrote that Judaism does not ask its followers to take a leap of faith. It asks them to take a leap of action. Although we may not know how to communicate with God, it is not true, as with so many other things, that the action follows the emotion. Sometimes when we act, we suddenly find that the action has swept us with it and opened new doors to emotional involvement.

Parents should ensure that children see them perform ritual actions. Learning by modeling is as important in religious ritual as in other human behavior. Children who see their parents read tend to grow up as readers. Children who see their parents practice tradition will know what it is to make ritual a piece of one's life.

These two themes, coming to God through people and coming to God through sacred moments, are not separate. The atmosphere of the home shapes the child's attitude toward tradition. How we look at the people in our home will profoundly affect those moments when we reach toward God.

Ritual can draw people together. It can help make a home into a place where love is given special, sacred expression. A harmonious home is the backdrop for spirituality.

The relationship between ritual and home life is important in another way as well. Ritual makes a point that is crucial for children to understand. In a home where the parents are religious, *they too are subject to the rules*. All too often children see parental rules as imposed only on children. They then believe that growing up means making your own rules and observing whatever you choose. For too many children, rules are something children have to observe. To be grown up means not to be subject to rules.

Not so in a religious home. I knew that my parents and I were subject to the same rules. They did not seem arbitrary because they did not originate with my parents' whims. The rules had a higher source. My father or mother did not have to fall back on "You must be here for Sabbath because I say so." It was woven into the tradition, it was a response to God. They had to be there, as did I.

This granted our home stability and coherence. It is very problematic for parents to force children to observe religious rituals the parents themselves disregard. When we do that, we are teaching two things: First, religion is just for children, to be discarded when they grow up. Second, parents do not have rules the way children do. And if parents do not have rules as children do, rules must be undesirable, since as soon as people can, they slough them off. Those are dangerous lessons. Rules are truly important to a stable home and to a stable society. They are as important for parents as for children.

Through good, humane rules, rules that are shared by everyone, we can build homes made sturdy by the dual pillars of love and tradition.

※ ※ ※

Exercise 3—Committing to a Ritual Meal. In chapter one we tried choosing a family ritual. One step beyond that is seeking to commit to a family time. A meal is the easiest, but family time does not have to be centered around a meal. The key is that the entire family must be present and the focus is on spiritual issues.

One of the best ways is to gather for a presentation. The children can put on a Bible play or sing a song relating to something they have learned about Judaism. Recalling what the family has to be grateful for that week can also be part of the proceedings.

————

LOOKING FOR GOD: MOVING FROM FAMILY TO COMMUNITY

There are certain prayers that cannot be recited in the Jewish prayer service unless there is a minyan—a quorum of ten people. Judaism understands that the way to God is not only through the individual soul, or even the family, but also through the community.

Central moments in a Jew's life are often community moments. Early on in life, the bris (circumcision) of a male child or the naming of a female child are public events. Religious celebration is not a private affair. This is another way of showing how seriously Judaism takes the idea that we are created in the image of God. For God must be present at sacred moments, and in some mysterious way God is more fully present when the community shares sacred moments.

That is why a wedding is also a community event. As a holy ceremony, it will certainly touch the lives of the two who are being married. But the walls of the *chuppah,* the wedding canopy, are always open: all are invited to celebrate. In joy, the community brings God into the celebration.

As we read the Bible, a pattern begins to emerge: it begins with individuals, moves to families, and culminates in community. The Bible begins with the creation of two individuals. That emphasizes how important is each individual.

It teaches us that every human being is related. Moreover, it reminds us that this single couple, like all couples, contains an entire world within themselves. The story of Adam and Eve at the beginning of the Bible lets us and our children know how valuable we are and how deeply we are connected to each other.

That is why the Bible can move so easily from individuals to families. Families are our most immediate connection. Most of the book of Genesis is taken up with domestic drama. At the very beginning of the story of the people Israel stand Abraham and Sarah. When God says to Abraham (in chapter 12), "Go forth from your land," this is spoken in the singular, as if Abraham alone is to go forth. But so ingrained is the ideal of family that Abraham never considers making a solitary journey. Along with him he brings his wife, Sarah, and Lot, the son of his brother Haran, who has died. When God says "you," Abraham responds with family. They are a part of him. Through family will Abraham be blessed.

The book continues with family dramas. Abraham is succeeded by his son Isaac and daughter-in-law Rebecca. In turn Jacob, Rachel, and Leah carry the tradition along.

These are not perfect families. Far from it: The range of problems that beset Abraham and his offspring include sibling rivalries, fights between parents and children, threats, broken promises, mistakes, and abandonment. Things often go terribly wrong. The Bible does not present an idyllic family life to which all should aspire. The families of the Bible do not live in Oz or Eden. Rather, we are taught that even though families are imperfect, full of different personalities and different aims, God still dwells within them. Abraham, at the instigation of Sarah, threw his child Ishmael out of the house. His other son, Isaac, he brought up to the mountain of Moriah as a sacrifice. If Abraham and his children, with all their problems, could be the bearers of God's message to the entire world, surely we can manage to bring God into our lives and our homes in some way as well.

When we read the Bible together with our children, we want to show how real people overcome difficulties, not that they never have them. Their own families are not the only imperfect ones. In the end, after struggles and bruises, things work out. In the end, people can rise above what separates them.

Families carry tradition through time. One of the puzzles of reading the Bible are those long passages filled with "begats." We are given the lineage of various groups down the generations. To modern readers, such genealogical lists are tiring. What is the point?

Surely one purpose of such lists is to remind us who really transmits tradition. Tradition is what gets transmitted over the dinner table. From parent to child, the precious legacy is handed on. God is part of the inheritance of each home. Rabbi Harold Schulweis once noted that a child spoke with more wisdom than she realized when, upon being asked why she believed in God, she said, "I guess it runs in the family."

The Bible does not conclude with family, however. When we finish the book of Genesis, we are in the land of Egypt. When Israel emerges from Egypt, they are larger than a family—they have become a people.

How did the people the Bible teaches about come into being? The formative experience of Israel is in wandering.

Israel wanders through the desert and learns about the harshness of life, its difficulties and dangers.

While they wander, they learn something else as well. They learn about reliance. They cannot survive in the desert without help. That is one reason why they are rarely called "the people Israel"—rather, they are called "the children of Israel." They are children of the wilderness. That symbolic name, that people are children of the wilderness, is at the heart of the Torah. It means that none of us is entirely capable of handling life alone. We need families, communities, other people who care to help us make it through. Finally, that we are all children of the wilderness means that we need a guide, a parent, a sovereign. To build a family is a beginning. To build a community is a next step. But each is incomplete without God.

✺ ✺ ✺

Exercise 4—Taking Your Family to the Community. There are activities you can do together with your children to show them the sanctity of family and community. One way is through cooking or baking foods for others in the community who may be in trouble because of a death or illness. Another is by inviting over a group of people to share one of the spiritual meals spoken about in the last exercise.

The aim of such exercises is to show your child that belief in God moves us beyond ourselves to our families and beyond our families to our community.

———

LOOKING FOR GOD
INSIDE ONESELF

The rabbi Menachem Mendel of Kotzk once asked his students, "Where does God dwell?" Thinking the answer obvious, one of them said, "God dwells everywhere!" "No," said the rabbi, "God dwells wherever we let God in."

There is one more place we must teach our children to look for God. They must look, to be sure, in the beginnings of things; in other individuals; in sacred moments; in the family; and in community. But it is also critical that each of us, including children, be able to look for God inside ourselves.

We can find God inside ourselves at all times, but most easily when we are at our best. In the movie *Chariots of Fire* a runner claims that as he runs he feels God. When we are fully ourselves, when we use the gifts given to us to maximum capacity, we come closer to the Divine.

There are experiences in Judaism designed to bring this about. Jewish study is supposed to bring the student closer to God. That is why study is often conducted aloud, in a singsong chant. It is more than an intellectual operation: It is a way of arching one's soul up toward the Divine and finding God inside oneself.

God is evoked inside of us when we demonstrate those qualities that we know God wishes us to exemplify in our lives: qualities of compassion and of conscience.

God is evoked inside of us when we work to understand ourselves and others. In Talmud, the rabbis explain how wondrous was the revelation at Sinai. They comment that the giving of the Torah was like a mirror. Everyone saw themselves, understood themselves better. They could see God in the image given of themselves. When we see ourselves more honestly, we find a clearer image of God.

In discussing the revelation at Sinai, the Talmud also states that it was so exalted an event that even the least person among the Israelites saw more than did the great prophet Ezekiel, who lived many centuries later. Rabbi Abraham Twerski tells of a later commentator who asks a logical question: If it is true that the least among the Israelites saw more than the prophet Ezekiel, why do we not have the vision of the least among the Israelites recorded in the Torah? After all, the Torah does not even tell us what they saw in this great moment, yet we have a whole book devoted to the visions of Ezekiel!

The answer is a revealing one. We know about Ezekiel because Ezekiel struggled for his vision of God. Those who were standing at Sinai were granted great visions without any work. And nothing we accomplish effortlessly can be as valuable as that for which we strive.

So when our children work to grasp something, when they struggle to understand themselves, we can tell them that in realizing their own ability, they are coming closer to God. They are realizing the godlike nature within themselves.

Children accomplish not only in work, but in play. Play for children can be just as deep, and as reverent, as prayer or study is for their elders. Play has been called a child's prayer. Play can be that important, especially when it involves the whole person and grants the child the sense of something deep and even sacred. At its best, play can bring a sense of holy joy. And "holy joy," wrote Martin Buber, "is the beating heart of the universe."

To help understand what it can mean to come close to God, we should ask ourselves some questions. Often, questioning our own experience helps us to recall what our children are going through and allows us to guide them better.

The questions at the end of this chapter are designed for children. But we can ask ourselves the same questions. Does the I–Thou encounter of Buber's match our own experience? When did you feel a sense of the Divine presence? For each person the answer will be a little different. By recalling our own spiritual experiences, however, we can help move our children farther along their own paths.

Are there special moments in your life today when you have a sense of God? Which of the categories we have discussed is most real to you? Natural beauty? Human interaction? All along the way we should be constantly examining ourselves to understand how we react.

Different people will find that God speaks to them in certain settings and not in others. Just as we all differ in body and in temperament, we all have our own spiritual constitution. Nonetheless, Judaism holds certain things as universal in God's feelings toward us and in our obligations toward God. These are the questions of God's love and God's law.

QUESTIONS TO DISCUSS
WITH YOUR CHILDREN

1. When in your life have you felt close to God?

2. Are there special moments in your day now when you feel close to God?

3. What sight in nature makes you feel close to God?

4. Have you ever felt as though you saw a spark of God in another person?

5. Do you feel as if you have a spark of God in yourself?

God's Love and God's Law:
What Does God Want from Us?
Why Are There Different Religions?

Rabbi Israel Baal Shem Tov told the following tale: Once a young man wished to learn how to be a blacksmith. He approached an older man, who took him on as an apprentice. Soon the young man's technique was perfect. He had learned all the skills of the trade. But when the time came to forge iron on his own, he was a failure. Turning with pleading eyes to his teacher, he asked what he was doing wrong. His teacher said, "You have all the information, all the tools, and you've mastered the techniques, but you still do not know how to kindle a spark."

CENTRAL TO JUDAISM is the idea that God loves us. Although we may be unused to this idea, much of Judaism follows from it. God's love is the spark that ignites the tradition.

Because of that love, God cares about how human beings treat one another. Indeed, goodness is the first demand made upon us by God. Law is a way of ensuring that we will have guidelines to treat one another properly.

We need law because it is not natural for people of any age to treat each other with consistent kindness. Judaism believes that all of us, from the moment we are born, have competing inclinations, good and evil, inside of us. So we must teach children goodness and not depend simply upon their natures.

Part of that goodness is showing children how important and fulfilling it is to act compassionately toward others. This includes not only those close to us, but strangers as well. To act with decency toward those whom we do not know requires tolerance, and in this chapter we explore how we can teach our children to believe and still be tolerant with others who differ.

Finally, in our attempt to be good, to repair the problems with the world, we often do wrong. The idea of sin, and with it forgiveness, is part of both God's love and God's law. Both should be part of our children's vocabulary and experience.

———

For many people the phrase *God loves you* is an uncomfortable one. We are not used to talking that way, and it embarrasses us. We have difficulty saying "God loves you" to our children. We did not grow up with that vocabulary or with the ideas it expresses. The concept of God's love seems particularly strange if we were raised in a home where God was rarely mentioned.

Yet the idea of God's love is common to both Judaism and Christianity. When we seek to teach our children about God, primary among the lesson must be this one: God is not hostile to you, nor indifferent. On the contrary, to be a child in God's world is to be loved. As parents, that message is one we need to learn how to transmit.

The Bible speaks repeatedly of God's love. God tells Israel (Deuteronomy, chapter 7) that it was out of love that God liberated them from Egypt to carry the message of God's sovereignty to the world. Many other biblical passages emphasize God's love. The entire biblical book of the Song of Songs is seen by the rabbis of the Talmud as a love poem between people and God.

The discomfort many feel with saying "God loves you" has a number of causes. First, saying "God loves you" in English poses a problem for Jews because English is a Christian language. English grew up in Christian lands and was influenced by Christian culture. So when we use words like "faith," or "love," or "religion," they have Christian connotations. When Jews translate even traditional Jewish phrases into English, they often sound Christian. The phrase *Our Father Who Art in Heaven* is the opening of a famous Christian prayer, but it is also the translation of the old Hebrew phrase *Avinu Shebashamayim*. For many Jews the problem with saying "God loves you" lies not in the idea, but in the language.

Yet English is our native language. No matter how familiar these terms are in Hebrew, most American Jews will have to learn to adapt to them in English if we want to learn to speak of God to our children in the only language most of us know.

The fact that "God loves you" sounds Christian raises another important issue. Children must learn to define themselves on their own terms. Just because an idea or a phrase is authentically Christian—or Muslim, or Hindu—

does not mean it is not Jewish. A phrase may be Jewish even if other cultures share the same idea. Jews, Muslims, and Christians alike have to learn to define themselves without worrying that they sound too much like one another. God's love exists in Christianity. That has no implication for whether the idea is to be found in Judaism as well. Our children should be pleased to know that the basic ideas of their culture are shared by others. God's love is the great universal concept.

　　　　■ ■ ■

Exercise 1—Speaking the Language. Many parents will ask their children, "Who loves you?" When the child responds, "You love me," the parent smiles and approves. In this easy exercise we simply expand that. Ask your child, "Who loves you?" and let her name you and then name others. "Who else loves you?" Let the list go on—include grandparents, the other parent, siblings, anyone who is appropriate. It is a good way to remind the child how many people really care about and love her. As a last step, make sure that God is included: "God also loves you." This is an easy game to repeat, and it takes some of the discomfort out of simply announcing, "God loves you."

Those who are unhappy with the phrase *God loves you* may introduce a Hebrew equivalent: *Ahava Rabah Ahavtanu* ("With a great love You have loved us"), a phrase from the morning prayers. *Ahava* is the Hebrew word for "love."

————

WHAT CAN IT MEAN THAT GOD LOVES US?

There are reasons apart from language why the notion of God's love is hard to talk about. What can it mean that God loves us? How do we know it? What are we saying to our children in telling them "God loves you"? And what expectations might we be creating that we cannot fulfill?

The first point to make is that God's love, like human love, is first and foremost an expression of attachment, not a promise of services rendered. We set our children up for terrible disappointment if we equate God's love with God's granting all their wishes. Love is a way of telling a human being "You are not alone. God cares for you, knows you, and understands you."

For children who feel at times isolated, this is a function of love that can be understood and appreciated. The feeling that children have in special moments—when they feel a hug around the heart—is an expression of receiving a sense of God's love.

God's love makes the world seem safer. The world is dangerous at times, but knowing God loves you can take the edge off fear. We do not want to encourage a false sense of security in children; but neither do we want them to see the world as an enemy. Because this is God's world, and God loves us, the world is at bottom a good place.

Finally, God's love is the logical outcome of God's creation. It is hard to believe that God would make us, endow us with the capacity to love and receive love, and not care about us.

Theologians may be uncomfortable with this sort of language. To speak of God in human terms is to reduce God's greatness to our own size. We cannot honestly speak of God's love the way we speak of human love. But we have no other terms to use. We cannot use divine language, for we do not speak "Divine." All we know is the language of human beings. Moreover, we are concerned with talking to children. As they grow, their understanding of love will deepen and with it their appreciation of what it can mean that God loves us.

To say "God loves you" is to say "The world is basically kind; you are never alone; even apart from all the people who love you, there is a God above whose love is all-embracing." "God loves you" means there is a love that will always wait for you to turn toward it, that will wait through the difficult times, a love that will see you home.

GOD'S LAW

Saying that God loves you is another way of saying something terribly important: that what we do is of passionate concern to God.

To love someone does not imply that you approve of all they do. In fact, quite the opposite. To really love often means that you are particularly critical of their actions. Children learn this early on with their parents. Other adults seem much less concerned with their deeds, good and bad, than their parents, who love them. At first children cannot quite understand why love means that one always has to be bothered.

Yet involvement is part of the meaning of love. We cannot be indifferent to the actions of those we love, even when they do not directly concern us. Our souls are bound together. So it is with God.

Much of the expression of God's love involves law. God cares about what we do. So Judaism has many dos and don'ts.

First we must take up the question of whether these dos and don'ts are really necessary. Why can we not simply leave children to grow naturally, to encounter and understand the world without restrictions? Aren't children naturally good?

ARE CHILDREN NATURALLY GOOD?

Judaism does not believe that people are naturally good. The way Judaism understands human nature is that we are neither basically good nor basically evil. We are basically split, struggling constantly with ourselves to behave well. We have impulses that pull us in each direction. Those impulses exist not only in adults, but in children.

At times we are tempted to look into the clear, cuddly faces of children and imagine that there is nothing inside but kindness. We call our children "angelic." They seem, so often, so sweet.

Indeed children are often sweet, warm, wonderful. But anyone who has watched a child grow up, taught a class, seen children on the playground, or watched siblings day in and day out knows that children also have a capacity to be selfish, to be cruel, to hurt others. Children sometimes treat each other with astounding heartlessness. This should not really shock us; we feel these unkind impulses in ourselves, and they were not suddenly planted in us at age twelve or twenty. Instincts of selfishness, even cruelty, are part of who we are. That is precisely why we should be so pleased when our children *do* behave well. We are pleased because it is *not* always natural to be good. We are proud of goodness because goodness takes work.

Judaism teaches that each human being is born with two impulses inside—*yetzer hatov,* the good inclination, and *yetzer hara,* the evil inclination. Both impulses are mixed up inside of us and are not easily separated. Sometimes the same ambition that leads us to push others aside also leads us to great achievement. Our drives are complicated and not easily sorted out. The bottom line is that for children, as for their parents, being good is not easy. It takes effort and resolve. Civilization is an attempt to set up a system of rules so that we can live in harmony and control the impulses inside of us. We should not be amazed when we see impulses in our children that make them less than perfect. That simply means they are human.

Of course children are sometimes morally ahead of adults. They are usually less scheming. At times children are readier to forgive and forget. And they can show an astonishing degree of tenderness that seems to spring naturally from their souls. In his book *Childhood,* anthropologist Melvin Konner writes that empathy "appears in the first year of life—much earlier than we formerly thought—and is almost certainly unlearned."

But we do our children a great disservice if we do not understand that goodness must be taught. We are not born loving everyone; we are born making distinctions. Look at a child who has been unpleasantly surprised by a new sibling, and you will see that not all children naturally love other people—even their own brothers and sisters! Unkindness, for better or worse, is natural to us in both thought and deed.

In time, that *can* change, and helping to change it is our task. Jewish law exists to help us rise above our baser impulses.

HOW WE TREAT OTHERS TOUCHES GOD

Traditionally, Judaism has divided religious law into two components: laws between people, and laws between people and God. The law prohibiting stealing is an example of a law between people. The law against blasphemy is an example of a religious law between people and God.

Most religious law is about the way people should treat each other. In the view of the rabbis of the Talmud, this was a part of the great innovation of the Ten Commandments.

When the Ten Commandments are enunciated, they begin with something that is not really a "commandment"* at all. It is really a simple declaration: "I am the Lord your God, Who brought you out of the land of Egypt." Two important lessons arise from this beginning.

First, we note what God does *not* say: "I am the Lord

---

* Indeed, in the original Hebrew of the Bible, they are called not the Ten Commandments, but the "Ten Sayings."

your God Who created the world." That would be the logical way to introduce so important a section of the Bible.

God chooses to mention not creation, but redemption. God speaks about the liberation of people and in terms of a direct relationship to human beings. These commandments are not coming from a God who is remote. They are not the product of a God who made a world and left. They are from a God who cares about you, who is close to you, who loves you; a God whose law comes out of love.

The second lesson from this opening is that all the laws that follow have to do with God. This may seem obvious, but until then in human history, what people did to each other had nothing to do with the gods. The idea that God cared about whether I hurt you was new.

This is really the basis for divine moral law. God cares about how I behave toward you. You are in God's image, and however I act toward you, I am in some sense acting toward God. In the same way that hurting the child hurts the parent, when we are careless of other people, we are behaving indifferently toward God. That is why in the yearly confessional on Yom Kippur, virtually all the sins for which we atone are sins committed against another person. The list mentions gossip, lying, bribery, and so forth, but each one begins, "For the sin which we have committed before You" —that is, before God. When we commit an injustice, it is an affront to God. When we sin against another person, it is God's concern as well. God is part of who we are and therefore part of all we do.

TEACHING CHILDREN THE MEANING
OF MITZVAH

The lesson for children is no different from that for adults. All our actions have a double consequence; they are directed toward people and toward God. In kindness, we honor God and please people. In cruelty, we hurt people and offend God.

Children should learn early the sense this entails not only of kindness, but of obligation. The Hebrew word *mitzvah* means not merely good deed, but a commanded good deed. Being good brings God into this world as it enriches human beings.

When I was growing up in Harrisburg, Pennsylvania, my older brother and I went on what we called "Shabbes walks" each Saturday afternoon. We would walk around the neighborhood and stop in the homes of some of our parents' friends. We were not stopping merely to chat. We were foragers—we were out for food, trying to trade cuteness for candy.

This began when I was six and my brother was eight. On quiet Saturday afternoons, Paul and I would begin our expedition. Some homes had specialties: one would feed us brownies; another grew tomatoes in the backyard; a third always had ice cream.

There was one visit we never failed to make. Some blocks away from our house there lived a widow named Rose. I was not sure why we always went there. The food was not as tempting as at other stops, and the conversation was almost always strained.

I remember Rose's apartment. It had heavy furniture

and a glass table in the middle. It was filled with small, ornate objects. It felt foreign to me as a child. There were few things to identify with—no bright colors or modern television. I was not always sure where to sit or what to say.

Yet when we came by, Rose greeted us with a peculiar emotion not shared by any of our other hosts. For the other people on our trip, my brother and I were something ranging from delightful to tolerable. For Rose we were necessary.

Rose greeted us with the enthusiasm of someone who had been looking forward to this visit for the whole week. The time we spent there, however uncomfortable, had a special quality to it. We left feeling better, and it wasn't because of another bit of candy.

For me this lesson came early in my life. In the course of looking out for myself, I came to recognize what it can mean to do a mitzvah.

Visiting Rose was a mitzvah. No matter how many or how few homes we had visited, it was a fixed stop. Though no one told us we had to visit, we knew we had to go. We realized, deep down, that we were being indulged by all the others who fed us. We had nice talks and we enjoyed each other, but it was a pleasantry that could pass. With Rose, we were giving something that was important.

When children do something wrong, they often know it instinctively, even if they cannot put their finger on what they did. When children do something right—when they perform a mitzvah—the same thing often happens. And the sense children get when *they* are needed, when *they* can do the mitzvah, lifts their souls.

The most extraordinary gift we received on those walks

was that despite our youth, we gave something that someone needed. The obligation was Divine; the action human.

In one of the most famous of the prophetic verses, the prophet Micah says: "You know what is good, and what God demands of you: Just this—that you do justice, that you love mercy, and that you walk humbly with your God" (6:8). The ideas are bound together: to Micah, doing justice and loving mercy are inseparable from walking humbly with God.

Micah's justification of goodness is in God. To do justice and to love mercy is to show faith. That is why the Bible in Leviticus, chapter 19, reads: "You shall love your neighbor as yourself. I am the Lord." To act with love toward others is an obligation because there is a God.

⬚ ⬚ ⬚

Exercise 2—The Value of Mitzvah. Giving your child a chance to do a mitzvah is terribly important. Children can contribute part of their allowance to charity. They can volunteer to help at various organizations connected with synagogues, churches, or charities. A very effective mitzvah for children is to visit someone regularly at an old age home who is alone. All of these possibilities, and many more, will teach a child how much he has to give.

Together with your child, choose a mitzvah. Let him or her understand how much they have to give and how it feels to give it. Stress that it is an obligation that you are just passing along—its origin is in God.

———

Giving a child a chance to do a mitzvah is bringing God into his life. He may not realize it at the time. But doing justice, and loving mercy, will bring one to walk humbly with God.

WHY SHOULD WE BE GOOD?

Do we need God to be nice to one another? One of the questions most frequently asked by older children (and their parents) is whether one cannot simply be a good person without God. The first answer is, Of course—one can be a good person and not believe in God. The deeper question is about motivation. *Why* should our children be good?

When a child asks "Why should I be good?" parents often respond "Because it is wrong to hurt people." If the child asks how we know this, we are a bit stuck. We can say that we know it from experience. Sadly, experience tells us it is sometimes pleasant for us to hurt people. Sometimes we gain from it—a fact that our children will certainly learn in time. We want to teach them not to hurt people even when it seems in their interest, even when it is tempting to do so.

If we say that only in this way can we become decent people, we are begging the question. On what authority is it important for us to become decent people? As adults we can entertain some sophisticated explanation. Society, we may tell ourselves, could not survive if everyone behaved badly. But what do we say when we want to give an individual child a rationale to act properly *now*?

What we want is an explanation that does not depend on human opinion. For if we argue that it is bad to hurt people because we say so, or because our parents said so, or the Constitution says so, all those human opinions could be wrong. There have been societies in which it was thought right to do terrible things to people.

Instead of sociology, or constitutional law, imagine saying the following: "It is bad to hurt people because all human beings are equal and they are all in God's image. To harm them is violating God's law and insulting God's image in this world."

No one can be certain precisely what God wants in every situation. To tell children, however, that God *does* want certain things is to make a very important statement: God cares about what you do. You have to evaluate your behavior not only according to what you feel, or according to what your friends or even your parents say; you have to try to understand how God wants you to act.

TEACHING GOODNESS

We educate our children to be successful in business and in social life. We take great care that they have the skills necessary to "make it" in the world.

We are not always so careful about educating them to goodness. We are proud of our child's artwork or test scores. Should ethical conduct be less important than these other achievements? To take pride in goodness is the beginning of sending a message to children: *Nothing* counts more than treating other human beings the way God would have us treat them.

The Jewish tradition has always placed great emphasis on

action. This is not because Judaism is indifferent to belief. The reason action counts so much is that Judaism teaches that what God wants is not just good feeling, but right action. To believe in God means to understand that our first responsibility is where the prophet Micah put it—first to do justice and to love mercy.

This is the difference between how we treat people and how we act toward God. The Talmud teaches "God wants the heart." When we approach God, what God wants is our soul, the heat of our emotions—our heart. To act without feeling when relating to God is to miss the essence of the experience.

But when we act toward people, how we feel is less important than what we do. Although it is better to practice charity with a full heart, giving grudgingly is better than not giving at all. The starving individual does not care so much if his meal comes with affection, as long as there is food. When we are young we learn to do many things by rote. We are told to clean our rooms or wash our faces even though we don't see the value in it. Gradually we come to appreciate cleanliness for its own sake. The same hope holds with goodness. We teach it in the hope that our children will come to be good not because they must, but because they realize its importance.

LAW AND TOLERANCE: DIFFERENT PRACTICES, DIFFERENT FAITHS

Part of teaching children about God is teaching them to act in a way that shows respect for the bit of God in other people. We pay honor to God by behaving honorably to human beings.

How do we show honor to those who differ from us? This is a difficult question for children, who grow so attached to their own customs and beliefs that they find it hard to understand how others do not share them. And if other beliefs are also good, why must our children stick to what they have been taught? How do we preach both law and tolerance to our children?

Once I was invited to speak at a Catholic university. Because of traffic I was late, and when I arrived after running across campus, my tie was thrown over my shoulder. I did not realize it as I launched into my lecture. Twenty minutes into my talk, I looked down and saw my tie was missing. After some searching, I smiled and pulled it back down off my shoulder. The class began to giggle. I suddenly realized what was going on. "You didn't tell me about this," I said, "because you thought it was some sort of Jewish ritual, right?" They nodded and laughed.

Those students were so afraid to offend that they would not even ask me why I wore my tie flung over my shoulder. Tolerance is a tricky business, especially when we are not sure what the other person's beliefs are. We need to teach our children how both to believe and to understand and respect others who believe differently.

What happens when we tell children that God wishes us to light candles and then they go to the houses of friends, or grandparents, and candles are not lit? How do we explain that others in our faith have different approaches or simply do not care? How can we explain that relatives are members of another faith and what that means?

In modern America this is not an unusual situation. The key is to teach a child the value of his beliefs without denigrating those of another—in other words, to combine law, love, and tolerance.

Children can be led to understand that something can be beautiful and yet not one's own. There is appreciation without appropriation. Children learn this when brothers or sisters have things that they cherish but cannot have. In the Aesop fable about the fox who peers through the vineyard fence at the grapes he cannot reach, the fox walks away concluding that the grapes must be sour. Part of being mature is learning the truth about "sour grapes"—just because one cannot have something does not mean it is sour or ugly. Things we cannot have can be wonderful and still not be ours. The beginning of tolerance is not denigrating everything that is not our own.

The reverse of that is that certain things *are* our own, and we should value them. We love them not only because they are good, but because they are part of who we are.

There is a story told of Chaim Weizmann, who became the first president of Israel. Before Israel was declared a state, Weizmann was testifying before a British government committee. One member of the committee said to him, "Professor Weizmann, why do you not simply forget the land of Israel, and ask your people to take some other land, say, in Africa, which would be easier for all of us?" Weizmann's answer was simple: "Sir, that would be like my asking you why you drove thirty miles into the country last week to visit your mother, when there are so many other lovely old ladies on your street." Your own home, your own family, your own faith, are not simply matters of convenience; they are *yours,* and that connection goes deep.

Once they have a sense that their faith is secure, children can encounter others' faiths with far less anxiety. You need not be worried at what others are handing out if your own hands are already full.

There are many ways to reach toward God. God may not wish all people to express their love in the same way. The world is fashioned so that different paths serve different people, and each adds something unique to the world. That means that different people worship the same God, but they use a different religious language, just as we can speak the same messages to each other all over the world, but in different spoken languages.

※ ※ ※

Exercise 3—The Variety God Made. With your children, put together an album of ceremonies. Find pictures of different religious objects or religious articles. Point out how rich is the tradition of human worship and ceremony. The book *The Circle of Life: Rituals from the Human Family Album,* edited by David Cohen (HarperCollins, 1991), offers wonderful photographs of hundreds of rituals from around the world.

Let your children feel how God is worshiped in many ways. Each discovery of a religious idea is finding out a bit more about God's relationship to humanity. Putting together your own "faith album" is a way of teaching your child that each faith has its own special relationship to God, but that none of them need threaten the special relationship the child feels is his as well.

———

This is the essence of the Jewish concept of "chosenness." It has never meant there is no other way to reach toward God. Even in the Bible, other people and nations have a relationship to God. As the prophet Amos declares in God's name: "True, I brought Israel up from the land of Egypt. But also I brought the Philistines up from Caphtor, and the Arameans from Kir" (Amos 9:7).

Rather, the idea of chosenness is that this is one special way of relating to God that Jews are convinced is important for the world. Understood that way, we can see that Christians and Muslims, too, believe in this concept of chosenness for their own faiths. To be chosen does not mean that others are not chosen for different tasks or complementary tasks. When a parent tells a child she is special, it does not mean that other children are not special in their own ways as well.

Our children deserve to be told that many cultures and beliefs in this world are beautiful—but they are not our own. Rather than spending time arguing the superiority of our own tradition, let us argue its excellence. Debates over the superiority of different religious traditions have gone on for centuries. Rarely do they convince or clarify. Far more often such disputes are a source of conflict, not a means of convincing others. What God wishes for us is to be good and to worship in a community and a tradition that lets us draw close.

Although God is often used to enforce intolerance, God provides a wonderful basis for building tolerance. The Bible teaches that all came from a common ancestor. To believe in a God means that each person can reach toward the Creator of all.

For if God is our parent, then all of us are children. This is perhaps the most unexpectedly powerful message that we give to our children. When children are raised with a concept of God, they realize that their parents are children, too —children of God. Everyone shares the searching, tentative spirit of a child. The Bible speaks of God using images of both mother and father. Human beings of all ages are in this together, seeking to connect to each other and to our parent: "You are the children of the Lord your God" (Deut. 14:1).

Throughout the Bible, the people Israel are called the "children of Israel." To be a person is to begin as a child and never fully to leave that state.

God's love allows us to be children even as grown-ups. One of the great myths of childhood is that one day we will wake up and be adults. When I was young I assumed that one day I would open my eyes and childhood would be gone. The symbol of that day in my mind was that when I sat on a chair as an adult, my feet would no longer dangle in the air. That day my fears would vanish, and all the insecurities and uneasiness of childhood would evaporate. As the years passed, the magical morning never arrived. I discovered an adult is often a child whose feet touch the ground.

When I was twelve years old, I went on a religious camp weekend with a group of men. I was the only child. It was the first time I had seen a group of adults acting "naturally" —that is, not adjusting their conduct to the presence of children. I was astonished to see how much they acted like children! They played ridiculous practical jokes on each other. They had silly fights and shamefaced reconciliations. They formed cliques and had rivalries. They were not a different species. These adults were like me inside.

That was disturbing information until we came together in the evening to pray. Then I saw that these adults were meant to be children. They were, quite willingly, children before God. They were momentarily shedding the weight of adulthood before a Presence so infinitely greater that they did not have to be ashamed of the parts of themselves that felt childlike, even childish. God's love was enveloping, and I understood the thread that runs through our lives, infancy to old age.

IS THERE SUCH A THING AS SIN?

A mitzvah, a commandment, is what God *does* want us to do. What about the opposite of mitzvah, sin? What about the things God does *not* want us to do?

One of the Hebrew terms for sin is *chet,* a word that comes from archery and means to miss the mark. It implies that a lot of what we may think of as sin is really a mistake, a miscalculation. This idea reminds us that the very heavy word *sin* should not be applied to every misdeed.

Chet is only one term in Hebrew for sin, however. There are other terms with more serious connotations. Sin is a religious idea with a place in our lives. It describes a grave offense against people and God. To murder is not a mistake or a misdeed—it is a sin. We should use words that tell us that certain actions are more than simply undesirable.

Teaching children about sin means teaching them that because we are in God's image, what we do has tremendous implications. We cannot dismiss people who do terrible things as "animals" and leave it at that. If someone is truly an animal, there is no reason to hold him accountable for his actions. Animals do not sin. An elephant is not morally to blame when it crushes a man.

Human beings are more than animals. That is why when they *act like* animals, it is so awful. What makes a Hitler such a villain is that he, too, was created in the image of God and horribly betrayed that image. To be born an animal is no sin. To be born a human being and act like an animal is a sin.

The concept of sin reminds us how important we are. We can sin because we are wondrous creations. We can disappoint God so terribly because there is some of God inside us. If we wish to teach our children how wonderful they are, we cannot hide from them the reality that being wonderful means having the capacity to be terrible.

The Jewish tradition teaches about sin using the idea of distance. When we treat another person badly, we create a distance between ourselves and that person. I insult you, and that verbally pushes you away. I treat you cruelly, and with that action I build a wall between us. I express love to you, and that overcomes barriers and draws you close.

When we offend or hurt a child, we feel the separation. And when there is reconciliation, the barriers melt. Everyone has experienced "sin as distance" with other people.

Similarly, when we sin we distance ourselves from God. To sin is to risk aloneness, from other people and from God. It is not the aloneness of courage, however. It is not a glamorous, "me against the world" sort of aloneness. It is the aloneness of someone who has not the boldness to connect to other people. Sin is a weakness, not an expression of strength. There is daring and drama in goodness. There is distance and sadness in sin.

In the Bible, sin is punished by distance. Adam and Eve sin and are exiled from the garden. Cain kills his brother and is forced to wander. Children who do something they know to be wrong feel the gap they have opened up between themselves and the one they have wronged. The desire to "make up" is the need to step over the boundary created by the sin and to come close again.

TEACHING ABOUT FORGIVENESS AND REPENTANCE

If we are to teach our children that sin is real, we cannot stop there. All people sin, for we are not perfect. Therefore we must also teach that forgiveness and repentance are real. In the Jewish tradition, repentance is called *teshuva,* a Hebrew word meaning "return" and also meaning "answer."

To repent is a way to return to the original relationship of closeness to God and to the person one has hurt. *Teshuva* closes the distance of sin. It is also the "answer" to the question of what we can do to renew and revive ourselves. How can we make up for what we have done? Repentance means that there is always hope.

Judaism is a faith that believes in the renewal and change of the human being. Change is hard, arduous; but it is possible. We can remake ourselves because more than anything else, what we are is a product of our own choice and our own work. Different people face different challenges, and it will never be easy to triumph over ourselves, but that confidence must never disappear. As the great Rabbi Levi Yitzchak of Bereditchev once said to God, as he stood before him on Yom Kippur, the Day of Atonement: "Dear God, I know that each year I tell You that this year I will sin no more. I know that then I go forward and, despite my promises, I sin. But I wish to tell You that although each year I believe I am sincere, this year, I *really* mean it!"

We must teach our children that a God who loves them is ready to accept their sincere pleas for forgiveness. "Though your sins be as scarlet, they shall be white as snow," says the prophet Isaiah (1:18). Having repented, the slate is wiped clean.

To repent of a *chet* (or a more serious sin), we need three things: *sincerity, a resolve not to repeat our deed, and an earnest attempt to right the wrong we have done. The three together are regret, resolve, and restore.*

The first step is to tell our children that, as the Talmud puts it, "God wants the heart." We must be sincerely sorry. *Regret* is the beginning of repentance.

The second step is to be certain inside ourselves that we will not repeat the *chet*. We must *resolve* to change.

And third is to seek the forgiveness of another, which involves trying to correct what we have done. As much as possible, we want to *restore* things as they were before we sinned. In Judaism, if we have hurt another person, we must *first ask that person for forgiveness before we turn to God. Teshuva* is also returning to the one whom you hurt and expressing your sorrow.

Teaching forgiveness is only a beginning. Even more important is modeling forgiveness. It is hard to believe in a forgiving God if your home is one where mistakes are not forgiven. Parents and children need to be forgiven by each other. Parents have to learn to ask for their children's forgiveness. They have to show children that they are ready to forgive. Hardness and pride must be put aside if *teshuva* is to have real meaning in our lives.

▓ ▓ ▓

Exercise 4—Modeling Repentance. Think about the three steps of repentance: regret, resolve, and restore. At what point in your life did you carry them out? Or was there a time you should have carried them out? In this exercise, parents go first, describing an incident from their lives. Having then modeled an idea of *teshuva,* ask your children when they feel they sinned (after describing the idea of sin as distance) and what they did about it.

Things done *between parents and children* are fair game and can often prove the most effective teaching examples. For younger children, use very simple examples. And instead of using the terminology *sin* to apply to a child's misdeed, you might use *chet,* explaining the archery reference; we do not want to label every playground fight a "sin."

Because there is *teshuva,* we know we are not meant to be perfect. If God expected perfection, there would be no need for repentance. The idea of *teshuva* is very comforting. We need not be perfect because God is—the job description for perfection has already been filled. We can relax a bit. We should demand of ourselves and others constant striving to be good—not fruitless, frustrating efforts to be perfect. When we stumble, there is forgiveness, because stumbling is always part of the human march to better ourselves.

Forgiveness calms the deep fear that we will find ourselves alone. Everyone will do wrong. Knowing that doing wrong will not cut the bonds between us and those we love eases some of the anxiety of this world.

Modeling forgiveness in the home is but one example of modeling goodness. How parents behave profoundly affects not only children's ideas of themselves, but their ideas about God. No sermon about goodness will touch a child's heart as much as seeing a mother or father perform an act of kindness. No discussion of *teshuva* will be as effective as taking a distanced child in one's arms and saying, "I love you." If our actions combine personal goodness with tolerance, we help the teachings of faith come alive.

God cannot simply be what we believe in. God must be part of how we live. Rabbi Yisroel Salanter once said that it is easy to proclaim God as King over the universe. What is hard is to proclaim God as King over oneself. For God to be King over us makes demands. One of them is that we seek forgiveness and grant it.

Forgiveness cannot be superficial but must be from the heart. As we hope for forgiveness, so we are ready to forgive.

Tikkun Olam—REPAIRING THE WORLD

Jewish mysticism teaches that God created the world with flaws. The world needs to be fixed, and it is fixed through human action. We are the menders of the world. The phrase *tikkun olam* means "repairing the world."

The idea of *tikkun olam* makes human beings very important. The state of the world rests on our shoulders. How we behave toward each other and toward God determines the fate of things.

God has left a lot of room for us to fashion our world. An old joke tells of a farmer standing proudly by his field of corn. A traveling preacher approached and said, "You know, you and the good Lord are partners in making this field." To which the farmer answered, "That may be. But you should have seen this place when God was sole owner."

Human effort is indispensable for the world to flourish. God seems to have done only what we could not: create life, implant souls, understand fully the workings of our hearts. Anything that we *could* do in this world, God has given us the chance to do. Primary among those possibilities is fixing its flaws to the extent that we are able.

How we behave toward each other and toward the world does determine what will happen to us. With technology and weaponry, with the means to profoundly affect the environment, we as human beings carry the fate of this world in our hands. What is true of humanity on a large scale is true of each human being on a small scale. We are each part of the great task of *tikkun olam,* parents and children alike.

God has made an interdependent world. All creatures are connected. We are partners, parents and children alike, all of us tied together and tied to God; what we do touches everyone.

All children wonder what they will do when they grow up. The possibilities seem endless, and doors do not begin closing until we grow a bit older. From early on, we should encourage our children to include ideals of *tikkun olam* in whatever career they choose. It should be something that contributes to the betterment of the world.

▨ ▨ ▨

Exercise 5—Talking About Careers. When you ask your children what they want to do when they grow up—and *why*—be sure to see if helping others enters into it. Are they already, at a young age, answering, "To make a lot of money and be successful"? If so, it is our obligation to tell them that there are many kinds of success.

———

We live in a society that promotes achievement of all kinds: financial, athletic, artistic. Parents must be concerned about producing children who are also wrapped up in goodness. We have prodigies of all sorts; many children are prodigies of goodness but do not get the same attention. There are children who in small, daily acts show that they have a passion for making the world better. Sometimes parents recognize that for the invaluable blessing that it is; sometimes teachers foster and encourage such goodness; sometimes, sadly, we pay more attention to the promising athlete or scholar, as though such skills were more valuable.

From our earliest days we should be taught that goodness is an obligation we owe to ourselves, to each other, and to God. It is difficult, and we will not always achieve it. When we do not, we owe ourselves and others forgiveness.

God, through love and law, encourages us to be better. We respond to this not only by conduct, but by communication. Speaking to God is important because it grants us strength to carry out the tasks we believe important in this world.

That is one reason why a discussion of goodness leads us to prayer. Yet another is to try to figure out how God *does* help us in this world. What can prayer mean to our children? Will it strengthen them? Does God hear our prayers? Does God respond?

QUESTIONS TO DISCUSS
WITH YOUR CHILDREN

1. Do you believe that God loves you?

2. How do you feel God's love?

3. Are there times when you feel you committed a *chet?*

4. How can we correct a *chet?*

5. Why is it hard to be good sometimes, and how can we work to be better?

6. What is a mitzvah? Can you give an example of a mitzvah that you have done?

7. Why do people believe different things?

8. Do people of different faiths worship the same God?

Prayer:
Does God Hear Our Prayers?

A story of Rabbi Levi Yitzchak of Bereditchev: One day in syna-
gogue, prayer was disrupted by a boy standing in the back of the
congregation. He held no book and seemed not to know what prayers
the congregation was reciting. The boy was repeating the same thing
over and over again, with great fervor. As Rabbi Levi Yitzchak drew
close, he heard that the boy was simply reciting the Hebrew alphabet.
"What are you doing?" he asked. "I do not know any of the words
of the prayer," said the boy. "So I am offering up the letters, and
praying that God will arrange the words."

CHILDREN HAVE A natural instinct for prayer.
Very early, they learn the various sorts of prayers that
we all share: praising God, thanking God, asking God for
things.

But there are many purposes to these different types of
prayer that we can teach our children. Prayer will not always
grant what we wish, but it can teach us what we need. It
helps us open ourselves up and understand ourselves. It es-
tablishes a relationship with others who pray and with God.

There are many ways of praying and many settings for prayer. Some are in the synagogue and community, some are solitary. Some involve set words, some are improvised. Some are sung, some are silent. There is a day set aside each week to explore ourselves and our world through prayer, the Sabbath, a "cathedral in time." It teaches us to pause, to appreciate, to teach our children that not only doing, but being, is sacred.

————

Our earliest prayers rise up spontaneously. Looking at the sky, we ask for help. We plead. We pray. Our prayers are like many of the prayers spoken about in the Bible, unplanned and heartfelt: "And the children of Israel were terribly afraid [of the Egyptians]. And they cried out to God" (Exod. 14:10). In moments of fear or of gratitude, we pray.

As we grow we tend to pray less frequently. Perhaps in times of crisis we offer up an awkward, desperate prayer, but we are not really comfortable with it. When our children speak about prayer we may approve of it, but we are not sure how to help them.

Children do feel the urge to pray. Prayer seems to arise naturally from life. Struck by the miracles of this world, we feel an urge to praise and to thank. In trouble, we ask for help. Prayer arrives early in life. Whether it grows with us depends on how well we understand it and appreciate its power.

Prayer is usually thought of as formal prayer with prescribed words and settings. That has an important place, but it is not the only way to pray. Any moment can prompt prayer. The rabbis in the Talmud imagine God saying as follows: "Recite your prayer in a house of worship; but if you cannot, pray in your homes; and if you are unable, pray in the field; and if this is impossible, pray while in bed; and if this proves too much, think of Me in your heart." Formal prayer is one way to God, but hardly the only way. More important than the specific framework of prayer is *that* we pray. One can pray at any place, and at any time, if the prayer arises from the heart.

When we teach our children to pray, we teach specific prayers with specific words. Prayerbooks are the greatest resource for prayers of the past. But any moment of life can provide an opening to prayer. Prayer can be planned, but it can also be immediate. It can meet the need of regular habit as well as the sudden yearning to reach out.

In most communication we are not certain that the other person is listening. We must wait for a time when they are present and ready to hear us. Prayer is the only form of communication where the other party is always present and ready to listen. In prayer we do not have to carefully explain our feelings. In prayer, when we are not sure exactly what we wish to say, or how to say it, we can simply look up, spread our arms, open our hearts, and say, "You understand."

※ ※ ※

Exercise 1—A Prayer Diary. Many people keep a journal of their thoughts and experiences. This exercise is about keeping a diary of your prayers. Encourage your children to note the sorts of things they pray for. Did they pray today to do well on a test? To have a certain boy or girl like them? For the health of someone?

The second step to this, as we will see below, is to look back over the diary and evaluate what we pray for. It is one way of seeing what we consider truly important.

TYPES OF PRAYER

The Jewish tradition recognizes different types of prayer. They pose different challenges. There are prayers of thanks, prayers of praise, and prayers of petition—that is, prayers that ask for things.

Prayers of Praise. When we teach children to praise God, we are educating in appreciation. "God Who does wonders" is one name for God in Jewish prayer. In praising God, we are reminding ourselves of the glories of the world. Since we know God through the world, when we acclaim God as "awesome" we are asking ourselves what in the world inspires awe. Calling God "glorious" tells us that we should see the world as an example of that glory. With each celebration of God we are exploring the world more deeply.

Prayer is filled with such celebrations of God. Prayerbooks constantly reiterate God's virtues, goodness, majesty. At first such constant repetition of praise seems overdone. Surely God does not need to hear all our compliments?

The purpose of praise however, is not to please God. It

is to educate us. We sometimes forget our limitations. By praising God, we remind ourselves that we did not make the world, and most of what we enjoy in life was given to us. The majesty of the world reflects back on God. When we teach children to praise other people, we are teaching them to respect the achievements of their fellow human beings. By teaching them to praise God, we spur them to appreciate the gifts of the *Ribon Haolam,* the sovereign of the world.

In praising God, we come to understand that *all we can offer to God is what God has given us: voice, heart, soul.* We work with God's marvelous gift to exalt its Giver. That is why every praise of God also leads to thanks.

Prayers of Thanksgiving.   Along with appreciation comes thanks. Perhaps no single attitude is more important to cultivate in ourselves and our children than that of gratitude.

People like to believe that they deserve the wondrous things that they have in this world. Adults who work very hard understand that their prosperity is a result of the work they have put into their careers and causes.

What is so easy to forget is that working can help you accomplish only if you live in an age and in a society where effort is rewarded. For most of history, that sort of society was only a dream. Even today much of the world does not live in such a society. Those of us who do are very fortunate.

We are fortunate because none of us can choose the world into which we are born. I did nothing to deserve being born into a loving family in the second half of the twentieth century in America. I could just as easily have been born in a famine-racked region in the Sudan, or in

Eastern Europe in the first half of the twentieth century. I was lucky.

The same issue of good fortune applies to our ability. One does not work to be born with a good mind or a talent for art or mathematics or language. These are gifts we were given. We work to improve them, but the raw material was given us. When a child finds that he is good in sports or she excels in acting, we have to remind them that they should be pleased and proud, but that such talents are gifts.

One theory many parents pass on to their children is that you make your own luck in this world. It is a theory popular among lucky people. But unlucky people realize that this is not always true. To be sure, much of what happens to us is a result of our own efforts, our own drive. But much of what we have is not earned. We are just blessed.

This is not a cause for guilt. No one should feel guilty for being fortunate. It *is* a cause for gratitude and responsibility. Children have to learn to give something back. We owe the world the attempt to help others enjoy advantages such as we were given. We owe God thanks for the gifts bestowed on us.

The Talmud teaches that "one who enjoys the fruits of this world without a blessing is like a thief." When we use something of this world, we should thank God who created it for us. Prayer is the expression of gratitude that we offer to God for all we have been given. It is a recognition of how much in this world that we care about, value, and take pride in is truly a gift of God.

One talmudic rabbi says simply, "I give thanks to God every day that I am able to give thanks." The need to express gratitude for what we have is great. When children discover that there is an address for the indebtedness we feel, it gives them a chance to pour out what is in their hearts.

One of the greatest blessings of life is to develop gratitude for what we have. In everyday life, gratitude helps sharpen our awareness of our gifts. Life is not boring or routine when we appreciate how fortunate we are.

※ ※ ※

Exercise 1A—Checking the Prayer Diary: Gratitude. Once you have begun keeping a prayer diary with your child, see if it includes not just requests, but thanks. What sorts of things have you both thanked God for in the past week or month? Are they similar? Do you notice, as you go over the diaries, that they help to develop gratitude?

———

In difficult times, prayer can remind us of how much we have to be grateful for. Understanding the magnitude of the gifts we have been given can help us through times when things are rough. We plant that resilience in our children very early on when we teach them to thank God for all they have.

Prayers of Petition. The Sixty-third Psalm begins, "A Psalm of David, when he was in the wilderness of Judah." The rabbis make a shrewd comment on this phrase. They note that although David later became king, no psalm begins, "A Psalm of David in his Kingship." When David is alone in the wilderness of Judah, in trouble, he composed a psalm to God. Later, when he was king, writing psalms had to take second priority to other things. We tend to pray, the rabbis are saying, when we are in trouble.

People do pray at other times as well, and those prayers matter a great deal. Still, prayer does seem to come naturally when we are in trouble or when we are in need. Most often when we ask if God heard our prayers, we do not ask "Did God hear my thanks?" or "Did God hear my praise?" The question is, "Did God hear my request?"

Children learn early that there is no direct, unfailing answer to prayer. The first time a child prays for a bicycle and doesn't get it, the realization sets in—God will not always grant what we want. We are then faced with the necessity of teaching our children about the difficult issue of whether God grants requests.

This question overlaps the question of why bad things happen, which we will take up in the next chapter. But it is such an important issue in religion and in life that dealing with it in two contexts will help clarify our thoughts.

I believe that we ought to make clear to our children that God does not rearrange the world to answer our prayers. What we attribute to God often has other causes. If we pray for one candidate to win an election and someone else prays for another, the victory of our favorite does not prove that God "listened" to us. The candidate's victory is due to politics, not prayer.

A common response to children when a prayer goes unanswered is to say, "God did hear your prayer—God simply said no!" That response seems to work when the child is asking for a new bicycle. When the issue becomes more serious, though, that answer becomes problematic. Did God simply say "no" to curing a child who is stricken with a deadly disease? Did God simply say "no" to a family that lives in a drought-stricken region of the world? The answer is clever, but in time it will backfire. We had better come up with a response that a child can understand, but that will also grow with them as they mature.

Different religious teachers will answer this issue differently. My own belief is that God hears our prayers, understands them, listens, and cares but does not intervene in the world to change the way things work. There are specific reasons why God does not intervene. It is not that God cannot—God is omnipotent and can do whatever God chooses. But God does not.

I have been driven to the conclusion by straightforward reasoning. Too many people throughout history, good, pious people, have prayed their hardest and not been answered for me to believe that God intervenes supernaturally in our world. When one person survives a terrible disaster and says "God had plans for me," the question is always the same: Does that mean God had no plans for the other five hundred who perished? Does God answer prayers only of those sitting in a certain building or speaking a certain language? It makes more sense to believe that luck has a strong place in this world, and we should teach our children that we do not pray to get specific goods, but to change ourselves and others.

In chapter 4 we spoke about Martin Buber's idea that it is important to relate to other human beings not just for what you can get out of them, but for their full selves. Part of the idea of prayer is to treat God, not like a gift store in the sky—or even like a Doctor in the sky—but as One who is prepared to enter into relationship with human beings. It is difficult to find a full relationship with God if our attachment is based solely on what we can get out of the connection.

Praying to God for specific needs can help us and comfort us. We run a great risk, however, if we teach our children that God will grant their wishes if only they are good enough or pray hard enough. For they will soon discover that people who are not good often get what they want while they, following their parents' advice, have not gotten what they asked for. If they understand prayer as a bargaining tool, it will not be long before they abandon prayer. Why should they keep praying if prayer is to get what one wants out of life and it does not work? But prayer is not for that purpose and does not work that way.

What are the aims of prayer, and how can prayer enrich our lives?

Prayer Helps Us to Understand What We Need. By asking God for things we believe we need, prayer helps us to clarify what we truly need. When we look in the prayerbook, we find the desires of human beings, which have been refined over centuries to arrive at what is truly important. A child who does not get a bicycle can still reflect on the prayer itself; is that what she should be praying for? Are there other things, more vital things, to ask for first?

This is one reason why we have a prayerbook. Children often ask why they cannot simply pray what is in their hearts. The answer is that of course they can, but there are other elements involved in a prayerbook. Not only does it connect us to a community, but it reminds us of what really matters.

Naturally, when we pray we often ask for things that are frivolous, or worse. How many sports teams pray for victory as though it were of concern to the Creator of the universe which team did well this season? By trivializing God, worshipers make themselves small.

We also pray for things that we should not have. As the Talmud so memorably phrases it, even a burglar prays for God's help as he prepares to enter his victim's home. A prayerbook can remind us what really counts and steer our prayers away from the trivial and the unworthy.

▨ ▨ ▨

Exercise 1B—Checking the Prayer Diary: Requests. This time we are looking to see what requests we have made in our prayer diaries. Are they worthy? Do they change over time as we examine them?

———

Prayer is less about changing the world than it is about changing ourselves. The Hebrew word for "to pray," *l'hitpallel,* is reflexive. The root means "to judge" or "to clarify," so prayer is self-judgment or self-evaluation. When we see what we pray for, we understand ourselves better. With prayer, children can begin the great process of self-knowledge, which is so important to a life of spiritual depth.

Prayer Connects Us to Others. In the Jewish prayer service, virtually all the requests are plural, not singular. "Heal *us,* that *we* may be healed," reads the *Amidah,* the central Jewish prayer. It is very rare to have a Jewish petitionary prayer that uses the singular. We do not pray for ourselves alone.

Judaism tries to shape us to think of ourselves as part of a group, not only as individuals. The rabbis remind us that one should always include others in our prayers.

God works through community. In the Jewish tradition, the synagogue is a called not a house of worship, but a house of gathering. You need ten to make a minyan, a prayer quorum, because God is best addressed by voices that rise together in prayer. When we request something from God, it is understood that there are others around us who also need, who are also in trouble.

There are some crucial prayers in the Jewish liturgy that cannot be recited if one is alone; only with a minyan can they be said. Among them is the mourner's prayer. For God's presence is made real by community. Though the mourner at times feels terribly alone, the people gathered around assure him that God is with him. By their presence, other people symbolize the concern of God.

An old Jewish joke tells of two men walking together to synagogue when they were approached by a third man. He looked at one of the worshipers and said, "Why are you going to synagogue? You don't believe in God! I understand why your friend Schwartz here is going—he is a religious man. But you? Why would you waste your time?" To which the man answered, "Schwartz goes to synagogue to talk to God. I go to synagogue to talk to Schwartz!"

That is not so farfetched. Children who learn to pray in a community learn that praying together creates community. Few things make a deeper impression on a child than to be together in a group of other children in prayer. Often we learn not by instruction, but by social relationships that let us find our own way. Peer groups can work with prayer, as they do with childhood sports and social skills.

Prayer heightens our awareness of others and helps create sacred community. It binds us to other people and to God.

Prayer as a Teacher.　In the Jewish prayer service there are passages taken from the Bible and from rabbinic literature. These passages are included for at least two reasons. First, they fulfill the idea that one should study at least some Torah each day. Second, they remind us that learning is a kind of prayer.

When we pray we are teaching ourselves. In schools it used to be a regular practice to memorize bits of poetry. People carried poems around in their heads, touchstones for the rest of their lives. Snatches of poetry would come back at certain moments, reminding them of beautiful ways of expressing something important. Prayer does the same if we learn how to pray in childhood. Regular prayer embeds beautiful and important ideas in us, creating a reservoir for later years.

Strengthening Ourselves and Our Resolve.　Praying together to God also helps us strengthen our resolve to help one another. When we pray together we understand how much needs to be done. Rabbi Moses Lev of Sassov was once asked why God permitted atheism in the world. He answered: Atheism is important because when confronted with another person in trouble or in need, we should respond as if there were no God; rather than ask God to help the one in need, we should take action ourselves.

The rabbis state categorically that "one should never rely on a miracle." By praying in community we remind ourselves that *we* need to take action in this world. We have God's concern and encouragement, but the decisive steps must be ours.

The prayer we quoted at the outset of this chapter was a prayer of distress. "And the children of Israel were terribly afraid [of the Egyptians]. And they cried out to God" (Exod. 14:10). We did not quote what the Bible records as God's answer to that prayer. Moses comforts the people, telling them that they are about to see God's great power work for them. God then says to Moses, "Why do you cry to Me? Tell the Israelites to go forward" (Exod. 14:15). Even at this moment, which precedes the splitting of the sea, we understand the essence of prayer. It is not to persuade God to split the sea—it is to persuade us to move forward.

I believe God does strengthen those who pray in subtle ways. Those who pray feel a change inside themselves. There is no way to show that it is God who produces this change, but for those who feel it, no proof is necessary. Like Elijah, we can hear God in the "thin voice of silence." We have to be attuned to the message and to the strength it offers. Prayer is one of the ways that we tune the self to become receptive to God.

When we teach our children to pray, we are teaching them to go deeper into themselves. They are learning about a part of themselves that they will not be taught about in school. Prayer is a tool for strengthening and understanding who we are by establishing a relationship with others and with God.

God's Concern. The most important statement made by prayer, petitionary or otherwise, is that God cares. Sometimes we call a friend not to change the situation, but simply to have someone who cares listen to our troubles.

In speaking about prayer to children, I often say, "What God does best is listen." To know that you are being heard is one of the great comforts of life. All too often we feel that no one truly understands or truly cares. More than we want a solution, we want a sympathetic ear. God understands. That does not make all the problems go away, but it does make them easier to bear.

WAYS OF PRAYING

How we pray says a great deal about the tradition to which we belong. But how we pray also depends upon our own temperament and our years. Children do not have the capacity to sit for as long as adults. Their patience is less, and so is their span of concentration.

Fortunately, some prayers are very brief. We can teach a child to offer up a short prayer. Prayer need not be lengthy to be meaningful. The repetition in regular prayer can be taxing for children, as it can be for adults.

Efficiency can be destructive, however. A soul blooms slowly, bit by bit. It takes time and training. The repetition of prayer can create the meditative mood that prayer requires. Repetition helps us enter a different part of ourselves. Prayer is about trying to teach children to establish a relationship, not to fulfill a minimum daily requirement. Teaching a child to pray is giving a lifelong gift.

That is why we should seek to recite prayers together with our children, in the synagogue and at home. One of the lessons of prayer is that we change ourselves not only by doing, but by being. By being "prayerful"—a state that takes time—we learn what it is to pray. The Talmud relates that there were rabbis who took time praying so that they might be able to pray. We spare no expense or effort in developing our child's other skills. It also takes time to cultivate a soul.

So although we should not insist that children sit still for hours in prayer (as if they could!), we must also realize that prayer cannot always be done in an instant.

❖ ❖ ❖

Exercise 2—Nighttime Prayer and Silent Prayer. Perhaps the best time to pray is at night. The magic of night helps to solidify the bonds of connection between people and God. A nightly prayer of few words can mean a great deal to a child. You can recite a traditional prayer such as the Shema (see appendix) or a prayer simply enunciating love for God. In time, children will become accustomed to nightly prayer and pray even when their parents cannot be with them. Perhaps they will pray especially when their parents cannot be with them and will feel some serenity.

———

Another way of prayer is silent meditation. There are moments in the prayer service that allow for meditation. Our lives are rarely deliberately silent. We are surrounded by music, talk, television. To choose silence is to choose to go inside ourselves.

Not all prayer involves set words. Joy, too, is a kind of prayer. "Worship God in gladness / Come before the Lord in exultation" (Psalm 100:2). Children have a capacity for joy—a talent for being happy. Delight in the world is itself a kind of prayer. In play, in the skits and songs children perform for each other and for adults, there is a celebration of God's world that is itself sacred.

Needless to say, play that involves parents brings a special quality to this idea. We can play with a prayerful posture. That means that when we share time with our children, it is not only fun, there is a quality of sanctity, of life celebration, about it. Play becomes an expression of a special sort of love. The central book of Jewish mysticism, the Zohar, speaks of people with spiritual hunger as "children from the chamber of yearnings." We are all children of that chamber—especially children themselves. Children who have not yet fallen into the trap of believing that there is nothing mysterious about the world recognize that each instant provides an outlet for those yearnings.

Speaking to God in these various ways can be difficult or uncomfortable. But as Heschel wrote, "The issue of prayer is not prayer. The issue of prayer is God." Prayer is about approaching God. Once we have resolved to reach, prayer, no longer an awkward subject, becomes the way in which together we can reach toward the Divine.

A DAY OF PRAYER—A CATHEDRAL OF TIME

Unique among the gifts that we can give our children is the institution of the Sabbath. One day a week is set aside. An ancient institution, the Shabbat divides time into the everyday and the sacred. What is its purpose, and how can we find meaning in it today?

The most beautiful explanation of the Sabbath I know is in Abraham Joshua Heschel's book *The Sabbath*. In it he explains how the technology of our society is concerned with the conquest of space. It used to take months to cross the seas—now it is a matter of hours. We move easily across distances that presented hardships less than a century ago. In turning on the television, we can see something occurring on the other side of the world *as it happens*. We can even hurtle in ships into outer space, exploring regions our ancestors merely dreamed about.

In the modern world, space has shrunk. Nothing seems quite as far away as it once did. But for all that we have conquered space, we do not live only in space. We live in time. The sands still run through the hourglass of our lives at the same pace whether we spend our time at home or travel through the world. It is not by conquering space that we will live meaningful lives, but by sanctifying time.

How does one sanctify time?

The origin of the idea lies in the history of the world and the history of Judaism.

In the Torah's account of creation, it tells us that on the seventh day God rested. God's resting is a statement that creation is not all of life. Stopping and realizing what one has made is essential, too. The creativity of God is a model for the creativity of human beings. God's rest is also a model for people who think only being busy matters.

The Sabbath is not only a product of the Torah's creation story. It is also a product of Jewish history. The Jewish people began as wanderers. They traveled through the desert. Much of their subsequent history was in exile. A people in exile cannot rely on structures to be sacred. They cannot build cathedrals to carry on their backs. They can, however, build a cathedral in time. That cathedral is the Sabbath. The Sabbath can travel with us wherever we go.

One day out of the week we lay aside the race to conquest. Instead of rushing, building, *doing,* we stop and concentrate on being. We live in the world rather than focusing on changing it. Instead of creating, we permit ourselves to enjoy what has been created.

Everyone who works knows the satisfaction of accomplishment. The Sabbath gives the satisfaction of being able to cease accomplishing—not out of laziness, but out of a decision to turn inward instead of outward, to exhale and let our shoulders relax, to soften ourselves. The Sabbath is the period, the rest stop of the week.

If we observe the Sabbath, we teach our children that the culmination of life is not work. The culmination of life is to be able to rest from one's work, survey with satisfaction what one has done, and live in calm space for one day. Our labor does not control us; we can stop. We can spend time with those whom we love and not worry constantly about the product, the market, the job. As was memorably said by a man who retired to spend more time with his family: "No one on his deathbed says, 'If only I had spent more time at the office.'"

Children understand the different feeling that such a day creates. In my parents' home, the candles, the white tablecloth, the atmosphere around the Sabbath, seemed to transform the entire home. It had become like a palace in time and not the regular home I entered each day after school. Religious scholars speak of "sacred space," places where the very air feels different. When we enter magnificent cathedrals we feel a sense of sacred space. That is what I feel when I enter a home prepared for the Sabbath. The rest of the week it may be in turmoil, but when the Sabbath arrives, a calm descends over the home. There is a peace built of sacred serenity. Such a peace lodges itself in the soul of a child, and few ever forget it. It is a peace that feels like the Divine presence.

❊ ❊ ❊

Exercise 3—Songs and the Sabbath. This exercise combines this section and the following section on speech. Children's spirituality and learning is often reached by song. One way of celebrating Shabbat is by singing together. Any children's bookstore will have CDs and songbooks for children (see further reading suggestions on page 234).

———

The Sabbath is a kind of collective prayer. By opening up a space in our lives, it enables us to pray.

THE MEANING OF HUMAN SPEECH

Words are very precious to the Jewish tradition, and no-where is that more evident than in prayer. Judaism's most important declaration is "Hear O Israel, the Lord our God, the Lord is One." We begin by listening and by speaking.

When we teach children to pray, we teach them the value and importance of what they say. Words reach to heaven. They comfort those around us. They express our souls. Very early on, children learn the power of words with their families and friends. With prayer they can understand that there is a holy dimension to words as well.

If we are to teach our children about God, we must help them learn how to speak to God. Human beings do not only speak to God alone, in silence, in their own hearts. They also speak together, in community, with others who are in need. Prayer moves horizontally, toward others, as well as vertically, toward God.

When the biblical prophet Ezekiel first encounters God, God tells the prophet, "Stand on your own two feet, that I may speak to you" (Ezek. 2:1). Part of relating to God is achieving an awareness of ourselves—learning to stand on our own two feet. We teach prayer so that our children become not dependent, but independent. But we are truly independent only when we know our limitations and when we can make connections to those who care for us.

In prayer, we seek to help our children grow both spiritual *and* strong. These qualities should flourish together. Learning how to pray is a good start.

PRAYER AS A BRIDGE

Some speak of spirituality as the feelings we have inside. If you feel in communication with God, you are spiritual. This is the *internal* model of spiritual.

Others speak of spirituality as something reflected in our actions. If we feed the hungry, provide for those in need, then we are spiritual, no matter our feelings. This is the *external* model of spirituality.

Both models are means to God, and both are important to our children. Clearly we want them to do good deeds—that is critical. Yet we do not want them to perform charity like automatons; they should understand the importance of what they do, feel its sanctity, so that they might continue to do good in the future.

How do we bridge these inner and outer worlds? One way is by prayer. Prayer springs from inside us. It wells up from the heart and reaches out to God. The end result of prayer is to move us to action. So prayer is an internal feeling that results in action. With prayer we can join what we should feel with what we must do.

Prayer is about communication and connection. It is how we lift our spirits toward God and place our spiritual arms about each other. Part of the reason prayer is so important is that from our first dawning awareness of life, we know that this world can be a cruel place. Sooner or later every child is touched by the question of why bad things happen to us and why people die. These questions will recur throughout each person's life. To these critical questions we now turn.

QUESTIONS TO DISCUSS WITH YOUR CHILDREN

1. When do you feel like praying?

2. Do you believe God hears your prayers?

3. What sorts of things do you ask for when you pray?

4. What kind of feeling do you get from the Sabbath?

5. Are there other things you do that give you the same feeling as when you pray?

Why Does God Permit Evil?
Dealing with Life's Hardest
Questions

During a discussion with children in Dallas, a child asked why God made bad people. I asked the children in turn why they thought God made bad people. They offered many answers: One said it was a mistake. Another child said it was so that good people could fight against evil in the world. Toward the end of the hour a girl raised her hand and declared emphatically: "God didn't make bad people. God made people. They added the 'bad' themselves."

FOR CHILDREN AS for adults, the question of why God permits evil in the world is a painful and difficult one. It is tempting to offer some answer that will explain away tragedy.

But the problem is that as children grow older they learn that many of the answers they were told by adults are not true. They recognize that the world is unfair, and prayer and goodness often fail to change it.

Our first responsibility is to try to be honest with our children. We need to explore with them why God designed a world in which such terrible things happen to people. We need to help them understand how much evil comes from choices made by human beings. And we need to present evil not only as a tragedy, but as a challenge.

———

Until the age of twelve, I held a conventional sort of belief about God, and I had not thought much about it. It was rarely if ever a topic for conversation among my friends, and few teachers raised the subject with us.

As part of the summer program I attended when I was twelve, we were shown *Night and Fog,* a documentary movie about the horrors of the Nazi death camps. It pulls very few punches; the scenes are explicit and all real. On film I saw suffering and the results of evil on a scale that was far beyond anything I had ever imagined. Not only the horror, but the enormity of the horror, overwhelmed me. I knew of the Holocaust, but it was an abstraction. To see the pictures paraded before me forced me to confront what had happened. The film was graphic, and when it was over, I was sick at heart and sick at soul.

I walked into that film believing in God in a comfortable, conventional way. Suddenly, and seemingly rather late in life, I had been forced to ask myself the great question about religious belief: If God is good and all-powerful, how could God permit such evil as exists in this world?

It took a long time before I could deal with this question in a way that made sense to me and enabled me to come back to faith in God. For years afterward I argued that because of the problem of evil, one could not honestly believe in a loving God. God must not exist, or not be the caring, powerful God I had learned about. I thought of myself as an atheist, because I could not overcome those pictures now frozen in my mind.

In time, however, that feeling changed. As I got older I was willing to reexplore the question of evil and suffering. Suffering was no less horrible, and the sickness of heart and soul in the face of evil remains. But God's place in the scheme of life seems different from the way it did when I first tried to figure out why, if God loves us, we live in a world of such pain.

In what follows we will talk about a possible approach to the question of evil; we will also explore how to discuss this question with children in a way that is constructive, while acknowledging the profound shock in their lives when they realize that the world, at times, is very unfair.

THE QUESTION OF EVIL

Dear God,
I got left back.
Thanks alot.

Raymond
(Children's Letters to God)

As with so many other issues in childhood, the first thing to recall about the question of evil is that although it is as old as humanity, it is new to each human being. Too often parents will respond with, "Who ever told you things were fair?" But a child who has suddenly discovered that the world is filled with pain cannot dismiss this as accepted knowledge.

For the truth is we are always seeking to tell our children that things *are* fair. We try to reward them when they are good and punish them when they are bad. We want them to understand that fairness is important. When they treat others unfairly, we reprimand them. Suddenly, however, global questions make us act as though the world were meant to be unfair and there is nothing more to say about it.

The question of evil is a painful shock to a child. There are few things as fixed in the mind of a child, especially a younger child, as the concept of "fairness." "It's not fair!" is the battle cry of the very young. Sometimes it seems that children have notions of fairness built into them, a natural expectation that the world will be arranged in such a way that ideas of fairness will be upheld.

Our responsibility when a child raises the question of evil is to take it seriously. It is the expression of the oldest and most painful subject of human history. But it is also an immediate crisis of trust for an individual child.

So the first step in reaction to evil cannot be an immediate explanation. It is one of comfort and of respecting the seriousness of the question.

IN ASKING ABOUT EVIL, ARE WE ASKING ABOUT OURSELVES?

Being taken seriously is the beginning of dealing with the question of evil. Because the question of evil is also a personal question, to ask "Why?" is in part to ask "Why me?" We wonder if the world is really indifferent to us, if anyone will care if we are badly treated. Asking the question of evil is also asking to be paid attention to.

Psychiatrist Viktor Frankl, author of the powerful book *Man's Search for Meaning,* once told a story about being awakened in the middle of the night by a phone call from a man threatening suicide. The man insisted that Dr. Frankl give him a good reason why he should not kill himself. Frankl racked his brains for reasons, drawing on philosophy, psychology, religion—all he could muster. The man was still threatening as the clock ticked toward the early hours of the morning. Finally Dr. Frankl persuaded him to meet at an all-night coffee shop in a nearby neighborhood.

The two sat and talked for a while. Once it seemed the immediate crisis had passed, Dr. Frankl's curiosity got the better of him. World renowned as an author and developer of the theory of "logotherapy," Frankl asked the man, "Why did you choose me? Have you read one of my books, or perhaps heard me lecture?"

"No," answered the man. "Actually, I have never heard of you. I was in trouble and needed someone. I just picked your name out of the psychiatrist listings in the phone book."

Frankl was a little surprised but still gratified that he had managed to help save a life. He went on to ask, "Tell me, which of the things I said to you persuaded you not to do away with yourself? Was it one argument, or the whole combination?"

The man looked a little embarrassed. "Dr. Frankl, I don't mean to offend you, but you did not have a single argument that really changed my mind. None of them were good enough to persuade me to live."

"Well then," asked Frankl, a bit exasperated, "why *did* you decide to live?"

The man answered, "I called you up in the middle of the night. You didn't know me at all. Yet you spent two hours on the phone with me and agreed to meet me in a coffee shop before dawn. I just figured that if my life could mean so much to a complete stranger, it ought to mean something to me, too."

Even when we cannot answer the question of evil to our children's satisfaction, confirming their own worth is part of the way toward an answer. The question of why bad things happen to good people is often an expression of fear—fear that the child will be alone, abandoned, in trouble. Frankl's story points out that the beginning of a response to the question of evil is to care for the questioner. With that concern, we have begun to build a bridge that offers reassurance.

What does it mean to ask the question of evil? Eleven-year-old Julie, whose father had lost his job at the same time that her mother became seriously ill, expressed it by telling me, "If I was God, I wouldn't let these things happen to me." Julie got at the essence of the question. If we assume that God has the values we consider good, then God's conduct is inexplicable. That is the mysterious combination: a God who *could* prevent evil but does not.

The reverse side of a God who does not help good people is also a problem for children and their parents. What can we say about a God who *could* punish evil people but does not? After spending a long time talking to a child whose parent had been murdered, I was struck to discover that he was almost as upset that his father's murderer had not been caught as he was at the loss of his father. The idea that another person could "get away" with such a crime haunted him. Not surprisingly, his plea was, "But it's not fair!" Evil is a question of God's love, but it is also very much a question of God's justice.

BAD ANSWERS TO GOOD QUESTIONS

Sometimes as parents we are so anxious to explain God's workings that we do not consider the implications of our answers. One of the most common answers to evil is that everything really is fair, if we only knew all the facts. It must have happened for a purpose, we tell our children—that is how the world is made. If someone suffers, there must be a good reason. Perhaps people who suffer did something wrong that we do not know about.

I have come across numerous examples of this in teaching both children and adults. Once, a sixth-grader, Annette, went through a horrible experience. She was with her mother at a shopping center at night and they were held up at gunpoint. She was terrified. For months afterward she had bad dreams. She and her mother went into therapy to try to untangle her emotions about the event. It turned out that a large part of Annette's problem was not therapeutic, but spiritual.

Annette was a deep believer. She could not imagine that God would allow something so terrible to happen to her without a reason. She had been taught that good people are treated well by God and bad people are punished. So she searched her life for something that might have caused this terrible event to come to pass. Finally she had it. She recalled that on several nights she had skipped her prayers. After thinking about it, she now knew why God had allowed this to happen.

We should not dismiss Annette's reasoning so lightly. Annette learned it from the adults around her. She knew that often when something bad happened, her mother would look up at the sky and say, "What did I do to deserve this?" Annette was told from very early on in her life that people get what they deserved, and if bad happens to you, it must be because you did something bad.

In many children, this self-victimization goes even deeper. People who work with troubled children know that youngsters who grow up in families where there is abuse, or mistreatment, often assume they must be at fault. There are many reasons for this assumption, but one is that stubborn idea that everyone gets what he or she deserves in this world. If you are badly treated, it must be because you deserve it. After all, God made the world and God is just.

We need to get rid of this idea. The first step to explaining evil is acknowledging that it is evil, not justice. *Not every bad thing is a punishment—it is often simply bad.* There *are* injustices in the world, bad things that happen that people do not deserve.

The mistaken idea that all suffering is deserved leads us into another error. If we really believe that good people are rewarded, that must mean that those who are rewarded are good. After all, if God rewards good people, then those rewarded by God must be the saints of society!

Do we really wish our children to grow up with the idea that people who are successful, who are wealthy or famous or talented, are therefore "good"? Are good looks and physical health a measure of moral worth? Do we want them to believe the reverse—that those who have not achieved success, however defined, are really "bad"? That is not the message we want to send. It is not true. No thoughtful adult could believe it, and we do not want to teach it to our children, either. What we achieve in this world is a function of many different things, and being good does not guarantee success or even happiness.

So when we say God rewards good people, we have to consider whether those who are apparently blessed are good. Some are, and some are not. Good things do not seem to be distributed according to any set plan.

Another problem with the theory that we get what we deserve is that it victimizes a person twice. Certainly it is *sometimes* true that we get what we deserve: if we are nicer, we are more likely to have friends; if we take care of our bodies, we are more likely to be healthy; and if we work hard, we are more likely to succeed. But it is often true that someone who is good and careful and kind becomes sick. Do we want to add to the sickness the burden of believing that the sickness is the person's own fault?

⁂ ⁂ ⁂

Exercise 1—Heroes Who "Fail." Movies condition our children to believe that good guys succeed. Too often in the media, heroism equals winning. This exercise is for parents and children together to find heroes who fail. An example would be Isaac Abravanel, who was a special adviser to Ferdinand and Isabella of Spain. When they decided to throw the Jews out of Spain during the Inquisition, he fought against them but failed. In the end, Abravanel led his people out of Spain and wrote classic biblical commentaries that are studied to this day. Other examples could include resistance fighters, such as those of the Warsaw ghetto, whose rebellion was finally crushed.

Not only the history books, but the daily papers as well, are full of heroes who fail. Paying attention to them—even compiling a scrapbook—teaches children that goodness does not always prevail but is still important to pursue. For they will learn that goodness does not really fail if it is remembered and if it continues to inspire us.

———

Every rabbi has had occasion to visit children in the hospital. One of the saddest parts of that visit is to hear children proclaim this strange theology. "God is punishing me," I was told by nine-year-old Marcia after a painful and ultimately unsuccessful operation. She had been told that God rewards and punishes everyone in this world according to what they deserve. When she became sick, the conclusion was obvious.

ARE WE GUILTY OR ARE WE HELPLESS?

Marcia's conclusion is obvious only if we assume God punishes bad actions. There are solid emotional reasons for this idea of justice. First it gives us a sense of order. We can comprehend the way the world works, because good people get rewarded and evil ones get punished.

Sometimes guilt is easier to feel than helplessness. When Marcia told me that God was punishing her for being bad, it allowed her to explain what was happening and assign a cause to it. She was not stricken mysteriously—she knew why God had done this to her.

Explanation helps us feel a measure of control. Just as children always ask "Why?" they always have theories about "why." Sometimes children are so keen to explain the world that they will seek any explanation rather than leave something unexplained. *One of the tasks of adulthood is to make clear that not everything can be explained. There are things we simply do not know.*

There was an impulse at work in Marcia even deeper than her need for explanation. If God could strike anyone, at any time, then she was never safe. That feeling of helplessness was more than she could bear.

If God had done this because Marcia was bad, she could be safe. All she had to do was be better, and God would protect her. If she could be good in the future, then she would not get sick again. In that way, guilt is easier to bear than helplessness. Guilt gives us some control.

But the sad truth is we are helpless, and ultimately it is healthier for our children if they know the truth. Evasions and fantasies only work for a brief time. When the child grows older, she will know that we have not told the truth. What can we do then?

I recall a public dialogue I had with Judith Viorst, author of many books for children and adults. We were talking about her wonderful book *Necessary Losses,* which explores the losses adults have to endure in order to grow. I asked what had been the most painful loss for her personally. She pondered for a minute, then said, "The loss of the illusion that I could protect my children."

Losing the illusion that life can be controlled—our own lives and the lives of our children—is painful. The realization of our own helplessness in the face of life is hard to accept, but it is critical to growing up. Otherwise we not only spend time trying to control that which we cannot control, we also spend time blaming ourselves for things that really have nothing to do with us.

When I discuss the question of evil with children, the first thing I emphasize is that their perceptions are right— often the world is not fair. There are reasons why that is so, but it is important first to affirm the truth.

WHY IS THE WORLD UNFAIR?

Understanding the unfairness of the world begins with exploring why we are here in the first place. Asking a class of children why God created us is an interesting experience. "God created us to please our parents," was the revealing answer of one ten-year-old boy in a class in St. Louis. "Because when we do what God wants, it makes our parents proud."

A child in Los Angeles gave me the answer that I believe in myself, in her own words. "God created us so that we can be better than God made us to start with." Behind that statement is a profound idea about why we are here—we are on earth to grow in soul.

People are here to be better, to grow, to realize themselves. That is why with each accomplishment of our children we are delighted. "Self-realization" is the purpose of life, but not just self-realization of talent, or career, or even relationships. Rather, self-realization is growth of soul, and that growth is what matters to God.

Now comes the second step of the discussion with children. If the purpose of life is to grow in soul, how does a soul grow? The most immediate example is how our parents seek to train our souls. When you misbehave, what do your parents do?

In one form or another, the answer is "punish." Parents seek to train children to be good and therefore discipline them when they are bad and reward them when they are good. That is how we try to shape souls.

Then comes the third step—what will your parents do when you are grown up? Will they still discipline you? No, answer the children. Why?

Sometimes the answer will be clear and funny: "Because I'll be too big then. They won't be able to catch me!" or "Because I'll have my own family." But in time we can coax the deeper reason from the children. Because when we are adults, we have to make our own decisions and take our own consequences.

And this is part of the answer to why life is not fair. Because when people do things, they have consequences. This is what it means to be a person instead of a puppet. It is true that every time we hit someone, God *could* reach down and stop our fist. Every time we shoot a gun, God could grab the bullet. Every time we drink and drive, God could pull the pedestrians out of the way.

But if we lived in such a world, nothing we did would

have any consequences. There could be no growth in soul, because there would be no learning. We would be a world not of people, but of puppets or robots.

That means that people are free to do some terrible things. When they do, God will not stop them. Because if God stops one crime, God must stop all of them. God cannot reach down and save the victims of one tragedy and let others die.

So God gives people free will, the chance to do what they want. Otherwise there is no good and bad. And if we have free will, we have consequences. Sometimes the consequences are of the kind we like, sometimes of the kind we hate. But they are ours in either case.

God permits people to sin. As we know, sin often consists of the pain we bring to others. If we could not hurt, we could not sin. Equally, however, we could not perform kindnesses for others. To have a world where people sin and grow and help, we have to have free will. And that means a world in which suffering is real.

▨ ▨ ▨

Exercise 2—The Three-Step Discussion. Try to reproduce the same discussion with your child described above. There are three steps:

1. What is our purpose in this world?

2. If the purpose is to grow, or to make the world better, how do we train people to grow?

3. In time, why do parents stop punishing and rewarding their children? Do they still want their children to be good?

———

The beginning of our response to our children is that bad things are a part of having free will. There is one more step —the game of fair consequences.

THE GAME OF FAIR CONSEQUENCES

"Why do bad things happen to good people?" When we ask that question we have to recognize what kind of world we are asking for. We have to play "what if." What if good things always happened to good people and bad things to bad people? What if the world was made so that each time a person stole something, he got sick or lost his possessions? And each time a person did something good, he got health or money? If we do not want bad things to happen to good people, that must be the kind of world we want.

But in such a world, there would be no good or bad people. Instead there would be a whole world of people doing good because they were afraid of getting sick!

Imagine telling a child, "Take that cookie and I'll hit your hand." Then the child does not take the cookie. Has the child been good? No. The child has been smart, or prudent, but not good. *Goodness means doing what is right without knowing the consequences.* Goodness means doing the right thing knowing that life might be no better, or even worse, for you than before you acted. As soon as we have a world in which doing good is always followed by being rewarded, there is no real goodness left. There are only people behaving in a way that assures a reward.

Child psychologists have done work that supports this idea. Professor Peter Salovey of the Yale Department of Psychology described to me experiments that are popularly known as "turning play into work." Psychologists invite children to play with their favorite toys. Gradually the psychologists begin to pay the children for playing with those toys. In time they discover that the children no longer want to play. The joy was gone when they were playing just to be paid instead of playing for the fun of it.

What do those experiments show? When something is intrinsically meaningful, when it has its own built-in reward, people treasure it. But you can destroy it by adding another reward. When a person is good, assuring they are always rewarded for their goodness destroys the drive to be good itself. What would happen if money dropped from the sky each time we acted kind? Acting kind would lose its meaning. It would no longer be acting kind. It would be making money. It would be "turning goodness into work."

What all this means is that for real goodness to exist in the world, there has to be randomness. God does not reward and punish. Evil and good things happen in this world, but they are *not* God's rewards and punishments. Some people are lucky, for which they should be grateful. Some people are unlucky, which should evoke our compassion, not our righteous condemnation.

How do we tell our children this? The rabbis of the Talmud put it simply. "The reward of a mitzvah is the mitzvah." The good that we get from the good deed is the doing itself, the feeling of having made a contribution to the world. Parents follow the same practice all the time. At first we try to reward children for doing good. As they grow, we expect that they will do good *because it is the right thing to do.*

The ultimate ideal of raising moral children is not that they will do what is right because a reward has been promised: it is that they will do the good regardless of what happens afterward, because they believe in goodness.

ANSWERING EVIL

The most important question about evil is not a "why" question, but a "what" question. Not "Why does it happen?"—we may never have a complete answer. We must emphasize to our children that more important than why God permits evil is what God wishes us to do about it.

God sometimes makes the most forceful statements not by intervening supernaturally, but by encouraging people to make a difference. In the Bible, Solomon says (I Kings 8:10–12): "God said His presence would be in a dark cloud." That dark cloud refers to times of difficulty and darkness. God is found then in the light that shines through us, through people who seek to dispel the darkness and make it right.

Most evil in the world is caused by the choices we make. There are things over which we have no control—diseases and natural disasters. But ask your children (or yourself) what has hurt most in the past day or two, and in all likelihood you will get an answer about something they have done or others have done to them. Before we lay evil at God's doorstep, we must examine our own actions.

Every schoolchild has learned that there is enough food in this world to feed every hungry person. Is it God's doing that all are not fed, or is it to God's credit that we have a world in which all *could* be fed?

Part of answering the question of evil is answering the fact of evil. Children who band together in community to help those in need are providing an answer to evil, both practically and theologically. If we see the suffering in this world as our task, it looks different. It becomes not just a tragedy, but a challenge.

Suffering and tragedy are real, but they are not all there is. The world is filled with people who overcome suffering and tragedy and cling to goodness. In order to manage goodness, we have to believe that there is a purpose to it, some meaning to our struggle to be better.

One reason for families and communities to carry on is just this struggle. Alone, it is too easy to be discouraged, for the greatest pitfall in the drive to overcome evil in this world is despair. It is easy for our children, overwhelmed by the parade of suffering on the TV news, by the constant sensationalized crime on shows and in movies, to conclude that the world is beyond help.

Parents have to provide the counterbalance. God's world is worthy and good. One of the reasons it is good is that human beings exert their energies to overcome the evil of the world. The great photographer Yousuf Karsh once said that character, like a photograph, develops in darkness. We have seen that from the darkness of the world some of humanity's finest moments have sprung.

We know that much of what seems at first to be bad can prove in the end to be good. If we did not have pain, we would not know when our bodies were in trouble. If there were no want, there would be no achievement. Sometimes deprivation helps us appreciate what we have.

There is an old Jewish folk tale of a man who went to his rabbi complaining that his house was too small. The rabbi asked him, "Do you have a goat?" The man was puzzled but said yes, he had a goat. The rabbi told him to bring the goat into the house.

A week later the man returned. He complained that his house was more crowded than ever. The rabbi asked him if he owned chickens. He did—and was told to bring them into the house as well.

In successive weeks he brought the whole barnyard into his house at the direction of the rabbi. Finally one day he could take it no more. He burst into the rabbi's office and said, "I am suffocating in my own home! Help me!"

The rabbi told him to remove all the animals from his house. The man brought all the animals back outside to the barnyard. On his next visit, he told the rabbi that he never realized how spacious his house really was.

This is a case where pain heightens our appreciation of our blessings. It is true that much of what seems at first to be unendurable can be made to be not only endurable, but educational or even helpful.

◼ ◼ ◼

Exercise 3—The Message of Fairy Tales. When you read fairy tales together with your children, note how in every fairy tale there is trouble to be overcome. The ugly duckling, the prince who was a frog, the slayer of dragons—all these stories are about trouble overcome.

For children, part of coming to grips with evil in the world is recognizing that it is often a spur to achievement.

———

Still, there are many pains and tragedies in life that simply cannot be viewed as ultimately good. In the end, perhaps all we can do is try to help.

There is a marvelous story of a man who once stood before God, his heart breaking from the pain and injustice in the world. "Dear God," he cried out, "look at all the suffering, the anguish and distress in Your world. Why don't you send help?"

God responded, "I did send help. I sent you."

When we tell our children that story, we must tell them that each one of them was sent. Each one is sent to do good, to help repair this broken world. That is not the task of an instant or of a year. The real test of a person is what they do not in a moment, but over a lifetime. Constancy, perseverance, and patience are what counts. Evil is a perennial challenge. It is our task to meet it.

It is our responsibility to tell our children that we hope they will live in such a way as to prove that God sent them. God sent them to make this world a bit better. God sent them to care, to help, and to love.

QUESTIONS TO DISCUSS WITH YOUR CHILDREN

1. What sorts of things do you see as evil?

2. Why do you think people do bad things?

3. How do you think God wants us to act when we see evil?

4. Why does God allow bad things to happen?

5. If you are good, will all good things happen to you?

6. Can you name something that has happened to you that seemed bad at the time but helped you become better?

The Bridge of Life:
Explaining Death to Children

A little boy once found a bird's nest that contained speckled eggs near his home. Fascinated, he watched it for a long time until he had to take a trip to the city. Upon his return, he rushed to the nest to see the eggs. He was shocked to find that the beautiful eggs were broken. All he saw were empty shells. He wept before his father and cried, "These beautiful eggs are spoiled and broken." "No, my son," answered his father, "they're not spoiled. All you see is the empty shell. The birds have escaped from the eggs, and soon they will be flying around the sky."

> Rabbi Earl Grollman,
> *in* Explaining Death to Children

WE WANT OUR children to be secure and stable. Yet we know that eventually the reality of death will touch them. When children confront death, their parents have choices to make. How do we explain this tremendous mystery? How much of the truth do we tell, and what words should we use?

Sometimes these questions are confronted first through

the death of a pet or by watching death on television or in the movies. Using these opportunities to talk, we can ease the way into a discussion of death.

When death does confront a child, we should have some notion of how children grieve and how we as parents and teachers can help them. Turning to religious teachings, we can explore together with our children the eternal questions: Why did God create death, and what happens to us after we die?

———

One of the gifts we try to give our children is the gift of stability. Even in our mobile society, parents know how important it is for children to spend as much time as possible in one place. We try to keep our children at one school. We encourage them to make long-lasting friends. Although families will change over time, we attempt to keep our family stable for as long as we can. We want children to trust the world, and frequent change makes people uneasy, even scared.

No matter how hard we try, however, one day children find out that this world has a drastic change in store for all of us. Children discover death. Everyone they care for, everyone they know, will one day die. They will one day die. Nothing is completely stable. No parent can hide the certain end of life. "Every true story," wrote Hemingway, "ends in death."

Death is a terrific mystery to children. But the mystery begins before children are even aware of death itself. Children are fascinated by things that appear and disappear. The game peek-a-boo is the most popular baby game of all time.

Significantly, the original Old English meaning of peek-a-boo is "alive or dead." Very soon children will learn that when things vanish, they do not always return.

Part of our task as parents is to help children understand death. We want them to know that death is real, and so is the hurt it brings. We also want them to know that the fact of death does not mean that life is not valuable. We need to teach them that adults struggle with this question, too, and we are there to help. Finally, we need to explore with our children the place of God and the possibility that death is not a final end.

HOW DO CHILDREN UNDERSTAND DEATH?

> Dear God,
>   Instead of letting people die and having to make new ones, why don't you just keep the ones you got now?
>
> Jane
> (Children's Letters to God)

Children's understanding of death varies greatly according to their stage of development. Developmental stage does not always follow chronology; maturation is a product not only of age, but of experience and natural attributes. What follows is generally accepted as the prevailing pattern.

1. Children Between Two and Five. At this early stage, the separation between life and death is unclear. Sometimes the dead are seen simply as "less alive" than the living. Many children are drawn to the connection between death and sleep and assume death is a longer, deeper sort of sleep. Death is, then, one more event, dramatic but not clearly final. Children of this age often ask when the deceased will return.

Studies on young children show they have a hard time coming to grips with the finality of death. It is also difficult for them to understand its inevitability. That all people will one day die is not yet an idea that a small child can grasp.

2. Children Between Five and Nine. At this age the finality of death is better understood. Children learn that the one who has died will not return. However, they too have a hard time understanding the *inevitability* of death. They believe people die if they get caught in a bad accident or get sick. The realization that *everyone* dies, no matter how strong or lucky, is incomprehensible. They know that death is the end, but many believe that it is an avoidable end.

3. Children Ten and Up. By this age many children can grasp the two great facts about death: that it will come to all and that it is the final end of life. Although these are hard to fully *comprehend,* most children at this age *accept* that these things are true. They do not expect a dead person to return. They know that others whom they care for will also die eventually.

Children of all ages may be unclear about what causes death. Often they believe something *they* have done or thought has influenced the person's fate. They may think that the person's badness, or even goodness, caused God to want to "take them back." Like adults, when children are faced with a fact of such enormity, they seek a rational, explainable cause. They have a very hard time with "She simply had a disease, and she died."

One contribution we can make to a child's understanding of death is to make clear that the child did not cause it. Sometimes when a pet dies, children assume that something they did or did not do was responsible. (Of course, this is at times true, but children believe it even without cause.) The same thought process occurs when people die. Children harbor hostile thoughts (as we all do), and when death comes to people at whom children have been angry, they frequently believe it was their own doing. This "magical thinking" is dangerous, and we have to ground it in reality. Bad thoughts do not kill people. Death is part of the design of the world. Our thoughts are not agents of death.

Some children will accept death far more easily than others and understand it better; the tendencies we have sketched out at various developmental stages are not hard and fast. People of all ages have within them bits of these different attitudes. A great deal depends upon life experience. Small children who have been around death—such as those confined for long periods to hospital wards—may have a more developed understanding. Adults who have been shielded from dealing with death may find its inevitability extremely hard to accept.

No matter the age of the child, there are important principles that we should keep in mind when teaching about death.

HOW MUCH OF THE TRUTH DO WE TELL?

One of the great mistakes parents make when confronted with death is to offer children simple explanations that will backfire later. Death is hard—hard to come to terms with, hard to explain. In seeking to make it easier, we sabotage ourselves by setting up future problems. Some common statements we should avoid:

1. He Is Going on a Long Sleep. Death is not sleep. A child who is told that death is sleep will spend a lot of time waiting for the person to wake up and return. We are just delaying the inevitable realization and causing them anxious expectation in the meantime. Additionally, after hearing such an explanation, many children may become frightened of going to sleep themselves. They fear they will not wake up, just as the person who has died has not woken up. When someone is dying, or has died, we should not hesitate to use the words *death* and *dying*.

The kind of language we use makes a difference. The phrase *passed away* does not mean anything concrete to children. Children deserve to be told the truth in clear, straightforward terms.

2. He Was Such a Good Person That God Called Him Back.

> Dear God,
> Do good people have to die young? I heard my mommy say that. I am not always good.
>
> Yours truly,
> Barbara
> *(Children's Letters to God)*

No one truly understands why people die when they do. One thing adults do know, however, is that whether you die young or old seems to have no relationship to your goodness; villains die young and so do heroes. And both sometimes live long lives.

When we tell our children that someone died young because he was good, we are frightening them out of goodness. Who wants to strive to be good so that God can take you while you are young? We *can* say that the one who has died was a good person, and we are sure that God will cherish him—but *not* that he died *because* he was good.

3. It's Okay—You'll Get Over It.

The grief of children is real, even if it is not always expressed. It is not okay—someone the child loves is gone forever. To tell them they will "get over it" is not helpful at the time and may not even be true. The death of a sibling or a parent can permanently mark a person's life. We should honor a child's grief by recognizing how much has changed, just as we do for adults who are mourning a loss.

The novelist George Eliot wrote that "childhood is comforted by no memories of outlived sorrow"—children are too young to know that even deep grief will lessen over time. The only way to find that out is to experience it. To demand of a child that he "get over it" will not speed the process. Indeed, it may hamper the process by alienating you from your child, as he may discover that his grief is not taken seriously.

Children often suffer in silence. To be quiet is not to be fine. At times children keep their fears to themselves because they do not feel safe. Children may be silent because they do not have the ability to express their fears. And often children are silent for vague reasons—reasons they cannot account for themselves. We should draw them out gently and not assume everything is okay because there is no evident fuss. Helping your child deal with death is an opportunity for the two of you to get to know each other in a different and deep way.

WHEN DEATH FIRST TOUCHES THE CHILD'S WORLD

Some children are introduced to death by the death of a pet. In some ways this is a great advantage. Painful though it is, the death of a pet provides parents and teachers with the opportunity to discuss issues that will be far more emotionally charged later on, when we are dealing with human mortality.

Exercise 1—The Death of a Pet. For those children who do lose a pet, a funeral can help explore many of the issues around death. The funeral can consist of a blessing, burial (if appropriate), and discussion of the memories the child has of his pet. It is a good setting to introduce God's place in the cycle of life and death.

Be sure to ask your child before having a funeral. Some children do not take the death of their pet as hard as parents sometimes expect. If they are deeply saddened, however, be sure to wait a while before discussing replacing the pet.

The first exposure to death in most cases is not with a pet, however, or with a real human being—it is with a television image. Death is a constant in the media. The problem is that television offers death without pain, without consequences, and usually without even the depiction of grief.

Seeing death in movies or on television does not necessarily prepare children for death in their own world. In fact, it may do harm, by suggesting that death is neat, artificial, and easy. Parents can, however, seek to use television just as they do the death of a pet: to open a discussion of death. When we watch television with our children and we see people die, we should not let it pass. Find out how they react to it and talk about how real death is different from how it appears on television or in the movies.

HOW DO CHILDREN GRIEVE?

Children grieve the same way adults do, which is to say in every possible way. Some children seem completely untouched by death, and others are plunged into deep depression.

I remember working in a camp with a nine-year-old child whose mother had died. One week after the funeral, the child returned to camp to complete the summer session. Her father told me that she had expressed no grief over her mother's death.

For weeks afterward, she followed the same pattern. The efforts of her counselors and the camp psychologist came to nothing. She acted as though everything was fine. Nothing would get her to talk about her mother's death.

One night, her counselor heard her sobbing. Throughout the night and most of the next day she cried. The internal dam had burst. With time and the patient help of concerned adults, the child's grief gradually emerged.

Our task as adults is to make it possible for that sadness to be released. Just because some children do not mourn does not mean they cannot. Some children do not know how to express their grief. To encourage them without forcing their pace becomes part of our job.

Children, especially younger children, show grief in very different sorts of ways. Sometimes they withdraw, at other times they daydream. Some children become nervous. There is no set behavior that all follow.

If children are unable to talk about their grief, it can be helpful to assure them that not only can they speak to you, they can also speak to God. God listens and understands. There may be feelings or ideas they would be reluctant to share with any other human being. It may feel safer to share them with God.

If they feel anger toward God, that is all right to express as well. Likewise, if you feel anger toward God for what has happened, you can express that to your children.

Children should learn early on that properly expressed anger will not destroy a healthy relationship. Parents and children cannot coexist without occasionally being angry with each other. The same is true for our attitude toward God. At times, particularly when one we love has died, we will be angry with God and perplexed over God's stewardship of the world. There is no reason children should not express that anger, together with you or alone.

The Bible provides many precedents for anger with God. Abraham yells at God when God plans to destroy the city of Sodom. Jeremiah and Job scream out to God over injustice in the world. And in the book of Judges, Gideon puts it simply: "If God is with us, why has all this happened to us?" (Judg. 6:13).

Even when children and adults feel the same things, a child's grief may take forms quite different from those of adults. Anthropologist Myra Bluebond-Langer writes: "Just as children can have the same concept of death as adults but express it differently, so too they can have the same feelings but show them differently. This problem came out quite clearly in the case of certain siblings of terminally ill children. Mothers became disturbed when the siblings responded to news of death with expressions of, 'Good, now I can have all his toys.' Later it came to be realized that this was the siblings' way of expressing anger with the deceased for leaving them (a feeling shared by the parents), of holding on to a part of the deceased (a desire of the parents as well), and also of expressing all the long-suppressed hurt at being neglected by the parent (a guilt felt by the parents)."*

The difference is not necessarily in the emotion, but in the expression. Sometimes we must decode our children's words.

In his writings on grief and loss in childhood, John Bowlby writes that children experience three essential stages of grief: protest, despair, and hope. Each stage takes time. The protest can be directed against God, the person who died, or other adults who remain. The despair is inevitable and perhaps the hardest for adults to confront. To see a child in depression or despair is agonizing.

The way out is to help that same child understand that life can be rebuilt. The loss will always be there, and memory is important. We do not want to teach our children forgetfulness, but we want them to have healing. We and God will remember. Hope begins when the child begins to build a life without the person who has died. Life is basically good, and we must go on.

* "Meanings of Death to Children," in Feifel, Herman, ed. *New Meanings of Death* (McGraw-Hill, 1977), p. 63.

HOW DO WE HELP
OUR CHILDREN GRIEVE?

The Jewish tradition offers advice concerning the way people grieve and recover from loss. The process begins when we first hear that the person has died. A blessing is recited— *Baruch Dayan HaEmet* ("Blessed be the righteous judge")— that affirms that although we are about to undergo a process of questioning and anger, at the deepest level we believe in the righteousness of God, whose decrees govern this bewildering world.

Judaism then proceeds to rituals of mourning and grieving that begin in intense grief and gradually help the mourner readjust to the world. At each stage we must ask what part these rituals can play in helping children.

Should children attend funerals of those close to them who have died? The consensus among child psychologists is that children from about age seven onward should be encouraged—but never forced—to attend the funeral. There they will understand how final the death is and have a chance to say good-bye. We understand how important that is for adults. It is important for children as well.

At funerals, children also begin to grasp the complex intertwining of life, faith, and death. They see the clergy presiding and have a sense that this is a realm in which religion has something to say. They see adults grieving and learn that the pain they experience is shared by others. Many children I have spoken to have had the same experience that I had in my own life—the first time I saw adults I knew cry was at a funeral. It made a profound impression on me. It showed the legitimacy of tears and the depth of their own sense of loss.

In the Jewish tradition, the funeral ends at graveside when the family and friends shovel dirt into the grave of the deceased. This is considered a great mitzvah, because it is the last service one can render. Since it is a service done for the one who has died, it is done without expectation of reward. The sound of dirt hitting a wooden coffin has a finality that emphasizes what has truly happened. Children too can participate in this final act of service.

After the funeral, there is a week of *shiva* (literally, "seven"). For one week the house is filled with visitors who provide food and companionship to the bereaved. For the difficult days following death, the house will be filled with guests, family and friends who listen and reminisce.

Once again, God is present in the activities of human beings. Comfort comes through friends. Healing is the work of human hands, but it is the Divine working through human hands. When people pray together, God works through community to console the mourners. Those who grieve are supported in taking the first steps back to wholeness.

The mourning prayer, the kaddish, is recited by children who have lost their parents. The kaddish is recited in a minyan, a minimum of ten people. The child understands that God's presence does not depart when the funeral or the week of *shiva* ends. God is always present in a community that strengthens those in mourning and consolation.

Children need to be included in healing, just as they are unavoidably included in feeling the pain. Indeed, there are times when the pain is primarily the child's, and adults have to explain to children something far more difficult than death in general—why the child himself is dying.

HOW DO WE TALK ABOUT DEATH TO A CHILD WHO IS DYING?

Seeing one's child in pain, and knowing that we are helpless, is extraordinarily difficult. Recognizing that we cannot protect children from all the perils of the world is inexpressibly painful for parents. At times it blocks our ability to give them what we *can* give when they are in trouble.

When children are terminally ill they are in desperate need not only of their parents' love, but of their parents' wisdom. Adults are the ones who have to help create some sense of meaning and purpose.

The first lesson is to try not to be afraid of what you and your child will be feeling. Do not treat them as though they are now so fragile that they have become china dolls and not living children. Be prepared to accept the power of their fears and of your own response.

When fear of death confronts a child, he is left with few resources in his own training to deal with it. Adults who face death have a lifetime of reflection to draw upon, and even then it is very difficult.

I have asked children to draw pictures of death. Sometimes the pictures are hopeful, filled with angels' wings and welcoming clouds. Usually, as one would expect, the images are foreboding. Almost always there is another being involved—an angel, a devil, a parent, a religious figure, or

God. Sometimes the figure is there to comfort. Often the figure is there to trigger death. It seems that most children conceive of death as something *done to* people. Children who are dying often wish to know who was responsible for doing this to them.

It falls on us to seek to explain that not everything that is tragic is a cause for blame. We can weep for what is happening, but there is no one on earth to point to. We know that God has made the world in which such things happen, and surely the child's (and the parents') anger against God is to be expected and honored.

Anger is but one stage of the grieving process. Psychiatrist Dr. Elisabeth Kübler-Ross has divided the emotions of those who are dying into five stages: denial and isolation; anger; bargaining ("If I am good, maybe God will give me more time"); depression; and acceptance. These emotions can be part of the grieving process as well.

It is our task to guide a child past anger to acceptance and to an expression of love for what matters.

One fear that we must address is the fear of being alone and abandoned. Some children are quite literal in this fear; to be put into the ground seems a terrible fate, and they worry they will be cold and alone.

Here is where it helps to begin to draw a distinction between their body, which is dying, and the soul. To do that we must begin to bring God into the picture as more than an object of anger. God can be a partner and comforter in times of need.

But in order to help that process we must discuss with

our children the most mysterious aspects of God and death: First, why did God create death, and what becomes of us after we die?

WHY DID GOD CREATE DEATH?

God designed the world so that every living thing dies. We cannot know for sure why it is that God brought death into the world, but we can speculate together with our children.

According to the Bible, after each day of creation, God sees that the world is "good." On the sixth day, after creating human beings, God sees that the world is "very good." In the Talmud, Rabbi Meir makes a strange comment on this phrase. He says "very good refers to death."

One way of understanding Rabbi Meir's comment is to say that value in this world is a result of knowing that everything is temporary. Could we love so deeply if we had an eternity to do it? Would we cherish things with as much devotion if we could do so next month, next year, next century—forever? Would we achieve anything if we knew we had eternity to complete any task?

One result of death is to urge us to cherish the beauty of what we have for as long as it lasts. In this sense, death makes the world "very good" by reminding us of its value.

This is a lesson that has to be taught delicately. Children should not live with the constant apprehension that what they love is about to be taken away. We need to give them the sense of stability that is the beginning of trust in the world. But the question of death does arise, and we should note that for all its pain, it can also help us appreciate what we have. To teach ourselves and our children not to take things for granted is also an important task, one that a discussion of death can help advance.

God made the world with the fall always following summer, a world in which things pass away. Death is certain, and we can only move the margins closer or farther. We are sometimes masters of *when* we die. We can cause or delay death. But *that* we die is God's choice.

God's place in death does not end with death itself. For the question that each person asks from childhood remains vivid throughout our lives: What becomes of us after we die? Did God create another world?

WHAT HAPPENS TO US AFTER WE DIE?

The belief that there is another world from which we come, and to which we return, is practically as old as humanity. Every religious tradition is preoccupied with the question of what happens to people when they die. As early as the Bible, the question is clear. "If a man dies, shall he live again?" (Job 14:12).

The classic Jewish summary on issues of death and the afterlife, *Gesher Hachayim* (The Bridge of Life), opens with an intriguing analogy. It asks the reader to imagine twins lying together in the womb. Everything they need is provided. One of them believes "irrationally" that there is a world beyond the womb. The other is convinced such beliefs are nonsense. The first tells of a world where people walk upright, where there are mountains and oceans, a sky filled with stars. The other can barely contain his contempt for such foolish ideas.

Suddenly, "the believer" is forced through the birth canal. All the fetus knew is gone. Imagine, asks the author, how the fetus left behind must view this—that a great catastrophe has just happened to his companion. Outside the womb, however, the parents are rejoicing. For what the remaining brother left behind in the womb has just witnessed is not death, but birth. This is a classic view of the afterlife—it is a birth into a world that we on earth cannot begin to imagine.

That is why an old rabbinic teaching says that birth and death can be thought of like the launching of a ship. People are apprehensive when a ship leaves, for they do not know what storms and adventures may befall it. When it docks back on shore, everyone celebrates. We do the reverse with people—we celebrate birth, although not knowing what life will hold, and we mourn over death. But death is really the return, the docking on shore.

▨ ▨ ▨

Exercise 2—The Miracle of Rebirth. This exercise takes a little searching but is well worth it. You are searching for a caterpillar. When you find one, take it on its original stick or branch and place it in a large glass jar with plenty of holes in the lid. Put leaves in and a few drops of water through the holes in the lid. With time and luck, you will be able to see the process of spinning a cocoon and watching a butterfly emerge. It is a dramatic demonstration of the idea of rebirth in another form.

WHAT IS IT LIKE IN THE WORLD TO COME?

Although filled with examples of belief in an afterlife, Judaism is fairly reserved about the details of life after death. It affirms an afterlife but tries not to get lost in speculation about what the afterlife is like. For Judaism asks us still to concentrate on this life. The tradition fears we will be so caught up in bliss to come, we will miss what is under our feet. Even though there is another world, this one is good, and this is where we live now.

The mitzvot are at the center of Judaism—because the most important thing is how we treat other human beings now, while we are alive, while we are certain of our world and our obligations in it. That is probably why the Bible is very sparing in mention of life after death. It is too easy to get caught up in hope for another world and neglect the distress that still exists in this world.

When children ask about an afterlife, we can affirm that eternity is real, but our task is to cherish and cling to this life. To avow life after death is an affirmation of a loving God who will not abandon us, even after we die.

When we begin to describe the afterlife, however, we run into all sorts of difficulties. In *Letters from Earth,* Mark Twain wrote that people imagine when they go to heaven they will lie on green fields and listen to harp music. They would not want to do that for five minutes here on earth, wrote Twain, yet they believe they will be eternally happy doing it in heaven!

Twain's joke points up part of the absurdity of describing the world to come. The simple truth is that another world is very hard for any of us to imagine fully. When we try to envision another world, we always make it up out of bits of this one: light, clouds, wings, comfort. We cannot really know.

Even more than uncertainty about details, we cannot know for sure if there is another world. Yet sometimes the question is urgent. Children are not always satisfied with "We simply do not know." When I have spoken with children who were facing death, either for themselves or in their families, their need is immediate. They cannot take comfort in philosophical abstractions. They need to know *now*.

What shall a parent do who has doubts or who simply does not believe? I think we must keep the door open. If God can make human beings out of nothing, why should God not be able to preserve us after our bodies have disintegrated? If God is a God of love, would God ever desert us?

Obviously to discuss this with a child is far easier if we believe in an afterlife. Then we can tell the children that we have honest faith that this world is not all there is. But whatever our private convictions, we should seek to leave the door open for the child to develop his or her own beliefs.

IS THERE A HEAVEN AND A HELL?

When children ask about the afterlife, we can expect that sooner or later the conversation will come around to heaven and hell. Graphic images of punishment capture childhood imaginations. They wonder what sort of world bad people go to and imagine equally the pleasures of good people.

Most religious traditions, Judaism included, believe that not all people share the same experience after death. In the Talmud, the most renowned of the rabbinic sages, Rabbi Akiva, says that the maximum punishment for anyone after death is twelve months. Other rabbis say that places of punishment and reward lie beside each other—that is, only one step separates one deserving of punishment from one deserving of reward—the step of repentance for wrongdoing.

As always, we have to listen to what is under the child's question. "Is there a heaven and hell?" can be another way to ask "Is there justice?" If the world's cruelest murderer and kindest person have the same fate after death, then truly there is no justice. Should not a murderer have a different fate from his victims?

Medieval maps prepared by the church often showed where hell was located geographically. You could literally point to hell on the map. Modern religious traditions rarely defend the actual physical existence of places of punishment. Yet the basic idea behind such religious notions—that there is ultimately justice, if not in this world, then in the next—remains.

When children ask about heaven and hell we can affirm that God, who loves, is also just. We believe that after death God weighs our lives and, in some way we do not understand, decrees that our lives influence our fate.

It is important to calm fears if the child is asking because he or she believes that some action will lead to punishment. Asking about hell can be a product of guilt over some action. This is the time to remind our children of the concepts of repentance and forgiveness. That is God's first desire on our behalf. To repair our misdeeds is better than to hide them or brood over them. Children should understand that to do wrong is inevitable; as Ecclesiastes puts it, "There is no one so righteous that he does only good and never sins" (Eccles. 7:20). The key is not to be sinless, but to repent.

Heaven and hell need to be stripped of their literal meanings and replaced with religious meaning. They are not places; they are affirmations of God's ultimate justice. In Hebrew the terms are *Gehinnom* and *Gan Eden*. Both form part of *Olam Haba,* the world to come. The name *Gehinnom* comes from a valley in Israel where pagan religions used to practice human sacrifice. So *Gehinnom* means a place where people are unspeakably cruel to one another. *Gan Eden,* from the Adam and Eve story, is a place that God has prepared. Where God is disregarded and people are cruel is hell. Where God prevails and there is peace is Eden, and we all pray that after death we may find ourselves in such a place. One rabbinic saying teaches, "It is not that the sages are in paradise, but that paradise is in the sages." For now we seek to create a paradise here, and we trust that God's justice and God's mercy will take care of us after death.

Exercise 3—If You Were God. How would you design the world if you were God? Would you include death? Would you give people the possibility to be evil? This is an exercise that is interesting to try at any age. As a help to stimulate discussion, you might look at Aryeh Kaplan's *If You Were God* (NCSY, New York, 1983).

THE AFFIRMATIONS OF LIFE AND DEATH

The basic affirmations that we want to teach our children are that life is good and worth living even in the face of tragedy; that God cares for our pain, even though we may not always understand God's actions; that we need to support and protect one another in times of loss; that God wishes us to be good and to seek to correct ourselves when we are not good; that God preserves the souls of those who have died.

Children learn early that nature has a cycle. Like the egg mentioned in the opening story of this chapter, life changes and renews itself. Children see the dead leaves of one season provide for the tree to grow the new leaves of another. All of death recycles in a renewed path to life.

Those who have died live on in many ways. They live on in our hearts as we remember them. The philosopher Voltaire said, "God gave us memories so that we might have roses in December." Even when the leaves have fallen, we can remember their beauty. To remind our children of those whom we have lost is a sacred duty.

Religion helps children cope with loss. It encourages memory, and gives us rituals to express grief that sometimes lies too deep for words.

"Childhood is the Kingdom where nobody dies," wrote poet Edna St. Vincent Millay. Sadly, no child can stay in that kingdom for too long. There is no way to remove the pain of death. Death haunts all of life, and we cannot shield our children from its reality. The best we can give in response is our honesty, our compassion, our love, and our faith.

QUESTIONS TO DISCUSS
WITH YOUR CHILDREN

1. What does it mean to die?

2. What do you believe happens to people after they die?

3. Do you remember the first time you thought about death?

4. Why do you suppose God made a world in which people die?

5. How does God help people who are sad when someone they love has died?

6. How can other people help those who are sad when someone they loved has died?

Reaching God Together:
Renewing Religious Life

A boy and his father were walking along a road when they came across a large stone. The boy said to his father, "Do you think if I use all my strength, I can move this rock?" His father answered, "If you use all your strength, I am sure you can do it." The boy began to push the rock. Exerting himself as much as he could, he pushed and pushed. The rock did not move. Discouraged, he said to his father, "You were wrong. I can't do it." His father placed his arm around the boy's shoulder and said, "No, son. You didn't use all your strength—you didn't ask me to help."

PEOPLE HAVE A spiritual hunger that ties them to one another. We try to satisfy that hunger in other ways, but in time it draws most of us to a life of attachment and community.

But finding a sacred community takes time and effort. How should we choose a synagogue, a rabbi, a congregation with whom to share our spiritual quest? What is the right atmosphere for ourselves and our children?

While searching for a community, we can create a more

spiritual home life as well. In family outings, trips, day-to-day interactions, God can be a comfortable part of what we are and what we do.

Ultimately we are seeking to enable our children to be the most they can be, not only intellectually and socially, but spiritually. A key part of that is the love we give them, a love that reflects a relationship not only between us and our children, but between each of us and God. In such relationships there is the hint of a greater love and a greater redemption.

———

The great Jewish preacher the Maggid of Dubnov once advanced a theory about why people spend their lives working for more money or for fame. He said that in each person there is a void that needs God. This spiritual void inside of us, said the Maggid, creates a hunger. Since we feel the hunger, we seek to fill it. Unfortunately we often try to fill it with other things: with work, with money, with power. None of this satisfies us. It cannot, because we are missing the real need, which is for God.

Many modern parents see the results of this hunger in the course of their own lives. They searched throughout their youth. Sometimes their searches took them on diverse spiritual paths: Eastern religions, offshoots of Western traditions, communes, or political passions. For some, the same hunger drove them to fill their days with work, with worldly success. In time, they settled into regular patterns of life, and many of their early, burning questions faded away. Now these former seekers have children, and they find that children reawaken spiritual hungers by asking questions long forgotten or discarded. They cannot ignore these any longer.

Many adults are returning in some form to the traditions that have understood and dealt with these questions for thousands of years. Knowing that the hunger is real, today's adults need to figure out a path for themselves and for their children to approach God. It can be done inside each family and by families banded together to help each other.

JOINING A COMMUNITY

There was a time when extended families, living under the same roof, made religious modeling easier. Parents and grandparents, and frequently aunts and uncles, were all around. The child saw many adult models of religious learning and piety. Now, most parents must bear that burden alone.

That is why for all families it is important to be part of a community. Synagogues, religious summer camps, schools —these are the places where children can be exposed to a variety of religious modeling. Parents cannot teach their children all the intellectual skills they need; that is why we send them to school. The same is true for spiritual skills.

Bringing a child to synagogue to pray is a way of affirming the importance of prayer. If we drop off our children and go about our business, we are declaring that prayer is important only for children—adults can dispense with it. Children will get the message that when they grow up, God becomes irrelevant. To go to synagogue *with* your child is to make a powerful statement: this is an activity that draws a family closer, gives it a sacred space.

When I was a child, my experience of family was tied to the synagogue. When I was young, I attended a children's service. When I got older, I moved to the adult service. It is not true that I was *never* bored. There were times when I wanted to escape and run around the halls (and times when I did!). But sitting beside my mother and my brothers, praying, listening, and sometimes joking, was a powerful family experience. And a powerful religious experience.

CHOOSING A SYNAGOGUE

Synagogues have different strengths. Some excel in children's programming; others are involved in community outreach; others have exciting worship services. Not all needs can be met by any one institution, and the same is true for a synagogue. A synagogue is run by people, and that means it will have the faults and frustrations of all human institutions. The synagogue is not a haven for perfect people, but a place where people seek to be better and to find sanctity in community.

In looking at a synagogue, see if its programs match the age level of your children. See what it can offer you as a couple, as a single parent—whatever your life situation may be. Some synagogues can provide support groups for families in need. Some synagogues have afternoon schools and some day schools. Some have day care, others provide short-term counseling. Each synagogue has its own strengths.

Find out how you feel about the professionals who work there: the rabbi and cantor, the synagogue staff, the teachers. Are they sympathetic to your situation and needs?

❇ ❇ ❇

Exercise 1—Revisiting the Sanctuary. The first exercise in this book asked you to go alone with your child to visit a sanctuary and feel the sense of sanctity. Now is the time to visit the sanctuary when it is filled with people. Visit a service and see if it fulfills the promise you felt when you visited the sanctuary alone.

While you are in the synagogue, speak to the worshipers. Ask them about the synagogue. Find out about their views and approach, and see if these fit your own.

———

It cannot be overemphasized that in choosing a synagogue, you are choosing *people.* They will have different strengths and reflect different ideals. Some will be loftier, others more earthbound. But faith has to be worked out in the human sphere. The French Catholic activist Charles Peguy said, "Everything begins in mysticism and ends in politics." No matter how noble the original impulse, politics is how we work through our disagreements, even in God's house.

One of the reasons there is politics in religion is that it engages people's passions, and that is important and necessary. There is a story told in the Talmud of two men who were walking by the ruins of an ancient synagogue. The first, seeing only rubble where a great building had once stood, said, "How much money did our ancestors invest in that place!" His friend corrected him gently, "How many *souls* did our ancestors invest in that place." In looking for a synagogue, or any house of worship, we are looking for a place to help us teach our children and reach our hearts —a place in which to invest our own souls.

When you go to a service, see if others approach you and make you feel welcome. Ask other parents what their experience has been in the synagogue. Strange as it may sound, "shopping" for a synagogue is like shopping for any other institution—you need to ask lots of questions. And take your time.

Synagogues vary widely in formality. Some require formal dress and stress decorous worship. Others are more free-flowing. Some do not mind children running free through the service. In other places this is judged unfair to those who are trying to pray. These are some considerations to weigh before you join.

In the Bible, in the book of Numbers, is a verse that reads: "And it was on the day when Moses completed building the tabernacle" (Num. 7:1). The rabbis point to an obvious problem with that verse—Moses did not build the tabernacle. Bezalel ben Uri is named by the Bible as the architect and builder. Why, then, is Moses said to have completed it?

The rabbis' answer is that stone does not make a sacred building. Bezalel was responsible for the design and construction, but a building alone is no more a sanctuary than a house is a home. Moses was the one who coaxed God's presence into the tabernacle, and that is what made it complete. It is not enough to have structure; a tabernacle must have spirit.

The same is true with a synagogue. It is a place of spirit, and it is the spirit that is most important to find. Facilities matter; personnel matters; but the spirit of the place is most important. Bezalel was responsible for the physical plant. When we choose a synagogue, we are in the steps not of Bezalel, but of Moses—charged with making the synagogue a place of spirit, a place of God.

HOW DO WE TALK TO OUR CLERGY?

One of the most important features of a synagogue is the rabbi. It is not the *most* important feature—that is the membership—but a rabbi sets the tone.

Remember that you are interested in teaching your child about God. To many children, God is represented in the clergy. How the child views his or her rabbi will say something about his or her attitude toward God. That is a heavy burden for a rabbi to carry, and parents should be aware of it and what it means.

One day in class, his teacher asked Barry if God can do everything. "No," said Barry. His teacher thought perhaps Barry misunderstood the question, so she repeated it. Once again Barry answered, "No." "All right," said his puzzled teacher, "tell me, Barry—just what is it that God cannot do?" Barry answered, "God can't please everyone."

What is true of God is far more true of the rabbi. People sometimes want their clergy to be superhuman. Rabbis, like other clergy, have a great range of expectations placed upon them. They must make a nice appearance, be kind, good, and well informed, be administratively competent, scholarly, and good with children; they must also be excellent speakers, good pastors, and family paragons all at once. This is just a sampling of the rabbi's responsibilities. Since no one can fill all these roles, it is up to parents to decide their priorities. What is most important to you in your rabbi? Scholarship? Pastoral ability? Talent as a speaker and sermonizer?

Whatever your choice, remember that the rabbi is there to help support the parents' efforts, not to take their place. No one can replace the religious education of a home. When we professionalize our children's spiritual training, we are all losers: the rabbis lose because they cannot do it all, parents lose because they miss the opportunity to help educate their children and themselves, and children lose, too, because learning about God from their parents is the most powerful way of all. Parents cannot teach their children everything. But they cannot abandon the task to religious professionals, either.

When you talk to the rabbi, ask what he or she thinks is important. Find out what the rabbi's energies are concentrated on in the synagogue. How many rabbis does the synagogue employ? (Many have two and even three or four.) What is the place of music in the service? What sort of sermon or instruction is involved? The more you can find out, the readier you will be to create a framework of religious instruction that involves the home, the synagogue, the community—all as partners in bringing a sense of God to your family.

OUTSIDE ACTIVITIES

Families take outings to teach their children all sorts of things. They will go off to attend museums and to teach them about nature. They can take outings to learn about spirit and about God as well.

I knew a man who, with no children of his own, made his home a sort of gathering point for children in his community interested in spiritual exploration. They would come together and sing, and he would tell stories. The stories always had a religious point, and sharing them with other children made them special.

Families can go on outings, even weekends, where song and story can be a part of it. Bible tales or other children's books can provide the themes. Children's songs or classical religious songs can provide music. Parents who think nothing of taking their family on a ski weekend might consider a spiritual weekend—or even incorporating some of this spirituality into a ski weekend.

We need a push to think creatively about ways to explore spirituality together with our families. God dwells everywhere, so there is virtually no activity in which an awareness of God cannot be made part of the mix.

FAMILIES TOGETHER

America suffers from the mobility of its citizens. Although mobility has benefits, it steals some of the great advantages of family. In previous generations, religious traditions were taught by extended families. In our day, families come in great variety, and sometimes we must create a family from friends, neighbors, and other people in our same life situation.

Not only must we make families, we must make neighborhoods as well. The neighborhood community is also a thing largely of the past. We can no longer count on knowing those who live around us or on being a part of each other's lives in any given neighborhood. But we should not let that be the final word on community. Even if communities are no longer "organic"—that is, they no longer spring naturally from the way we live—we can create them.

That is part of the popularity of the *chavurah* (fellowship) movement in Judaism, a movement that has parallels in other faiths. A *chavurah* is a group of families or individuals who band together for study, song, travel, friendship—all the features that families and in-built communities performed in the past.

A *chavurah* can help extend the family you have. Many *chavurot* (plural of *chavurah*) go on trips together, invite speakers, literally create their own community. Single parents and couples mix together in a larger communal unit. It is a way of bringing spirit into our lives as well as combating the isolation that is a part of much modern living.

WHAT WE HOPE FOR OUR CHILDREN

It was an ancient Jewish custom for parents to plant a tree when a child was born. When the boy or girl grew up and was to be married, the parents would weave together the branches of the two trees to make a *chuppah*, a wedding canopy. The symbolism was not only one of joining two lives—it also showed that the roots planted at the beginning of the child's life were what brought him or her to this moment.

The social training we give children determines their relationships. But spiritual training is also a root that has branches. One of the reasons we create spiritual communities is that by reaching out to God, we teach our children how to join others in a community of belief, of sanctity. They will join many associations in their lives; but few, if any, apart from a religious organization, will teach them to regard others as holy.

Not only does the synagogue teach children to regard their fellow human beings as holy, it is also one of the few organizations in American life where one can find people of all ages in one place. The ten-year-old can worship next to a ninety-year-old in the same sanctuary. In the rest of society we segregate the ages, forgetting that God's reflection is as visible on a face weathered by age as on a face fresh with youth.

We hope that our children are spiritually involved. We hope they recognize all types of people as holy. And we hope that our children fulfill as much of their potential as is possible in their lives. There is a story about the renowned Rabbi Zusya, who as he was dying began softly to weep before the disciples gathered around his bed. "Why do you weep?" they asked. "Because I am afraid," said Rabbi Zusya. "I am afraid of what God will ask me when I die. I know God will not ask me, 'Why were you not like Abraham?'—for who am I next to the man who first recognized the Almighty? And I know God will not ask me, 'Why were you not like Moses?'—after all, I am not a great prophet or leader. But when God looks upon me and says, 'Zusya, my child—why were you not Zusya?' What shall I say then?''

God asks each of us to be as fully ourselves as we can. But in order to do that, we must find a relationship with God and help our children do the same.

※ ※ ※

Exercise 2—Writing a Letter to God. For this final exercise, encourage your children to write their own letters to God. Invite them to write letters dealing with the questions we have raised in this book.

BRINGING THE MESSIAH

There are many interpretations of the meaning of the Messiah in Jewish history. Some concentrate more on a personality, a messianic redeemer. Others focus on a messianic age —a time when the world will be repaired.

The second chapter of this book began with a story about my brother Danny opening the door for Elijah on the night of Passover. There I alluded to an ancient Jewish tradition—that Elijah will announce the Messiah. By understanding why Elijah fits that role, we can learn something vital about what messianism really means.

Elijah in the Bible is a zealot for God. Indeed in one passage, the rabbis take Elijah to task, insisting that he was a zealot for the honor of God but not so careful about the honor of human beings. For Elijah often derided people for not being faithful enough.

In time, however, Elijah learned that being an isolated zealot will not change the world. Only among people could he make a difference. So when Elijah left this earth, carried in a chariot up to the heavens, he gently dropped his cloak so that his disciple, Elisha, might don the mantle of the prophet and carry on Elijah's work. Elijah had come to realize that without people to remember and care for you, zealousness for God was empty.

According to Jewish tradition, there are three times during the year when Elijah is expected to return. The Passover is one time, as we mentioned. Another is the end of the Sabbath, when everyone gathers around a candle, with spices and wine, to perform the havdalah, the ceremony that separates the Sabbath from the rest of the week. The third time is during a bris, when a child is circumcised. At a bris there is a *kiseh eliyahu,* a chair for Elijah.

What ties together all these occasions is that they are family times. The Passover, the end of the Sabbath, and the bris are times when the entire family gathers together. Perhaps it is not surprising that it is at such moments Elijah is expected.

There is a biblical verse, from the book of Malachi, that tells us what will happen when Elijah comes. The verse reads: "Behold I send the prophet Elijah to you before the coming of the awesome, great day of the Lord. He shall turn the hearts of parents to their children, and the hearts of children to their parents" (Mal. 3:23,24).

What does it mean that Elijah brings the Messiah? That family life is brought closer and made deeper. That love—the hearts of parents and children—is strengthened. And what does it mean, as several commentators have pointed out, that the verse reads, "Behold I *send*"—in the present tense? Elijah comes at every minute, every time parents and children turn to one another in love.

Speaking to children about God is not an easy task. But at each moment in our lives we have the opportunity to do more than simply teach and reach out to our children. We have a chance to give them a love not only deep, but sanctified. Such a love ties people to one another and ties all of us to God. That love may not in itself be the messianic age, but surely it serves to bring the Messiah one step closer.

"And all your children shall be taught of the Lord; and great shall be the peace of your children" (Isa. 54:13).

QUESTIONS TO DISCUSS
WITH YOUR CHILDREN

1. What do you like about synagogue?

2. What do you dislike about synagogue? How could the synagogue be made better?

3. What sorts of things could our family do together that would bring us closer to God?

4. When you think about the Messiah, what do you imagine will happen when the Messiah comes?

Appendix

Sample Blessings to Try

For Friday Night Candlelighting

English: Blessed are You, O Lord our God, King of the Universe, who has sanctified us with Your commandments, and commanded us to kindle the Sabbath lights.

Hebrew Transliteration: *Baruch atah Adonai, Eloheinu melech ha'olam, asher kidshanu b'mitzvotav v'tzivanu l'ihadlik ner shel Shabbat.*

For Blessing over the Bread

English: Blessed are You, O Lord our God, King of the Universe, who brings bread forth from the earth.

Hebrew Transliteration: *Baruch atah Adonai, Eloheinu melech ha'olam, hamotzi lechem min ha'aretz.*

Upon Waking in the Morning

English: I am grateful to You, Everlasting King, who has mercifully restored my soul to me; great is Your faithfulness. Hebrew Transliteration: *Modeh* (Females: *Modah*) *ani lifanechah, melech chai v'kayom, sh'hechezartah be nishmahti b'chemlah, rabah emunatechah.*

The Shema—First Line

English: Hear O Israel, the Lord our God, the Lord is One. Hebrew Transliteration: *Shema Yisrael, Adonai Eloheinu, Adonai echad.*

Commonly Asked
Questions and Where to
Look for Answers

Prayer

Does God answer prayers? (pp. 151–53)

What do you ask God for when you pray? (pp. 150, 153–54)

Do I have to be in the synagogue to pray? (pp. 145–46)

How does prayer help us? (pp. 153–58)

What are the different ways we can pray? (pp. 158–63)

Looking for God

If someone said "Where do I look for God?" what would you say? (chap. 4)

What does it mean that we are "in the image of God"? (pp. 35–37, 90–99, 109–11)

How do we see God in ritual? (pp. 18–22, 99–105)

How do we see God in the world? (pp. 41–43)

The Importance of Goodness

What is the most important thing God has taught people? (pp.121–22)

Why should we be good? (pp. 126–27)

Evil

Are people basically good? (pp. 119–21)
Why does God allow bad things to happen? (pp. 178–83)
Are bad people punished and are good people rewarded?
    (pp. 173–76)
How should we react to evil? (pp. 183–86)

Other Questions

What is holiness? (pp. 5–6)
How can there be different religions, and do they all wor-
    ship the same God? (pp. 128–32)
What is a blessing? (pp. 44–46)
Can we do anything to bring the Messiah closer? (pp. 225–
    27)

For Further Reading

A number of books are available to help parents and teachers pursue the themes in this book. Below is a just a sampling of the available reading.

For teaching God to your children, Harold S. Kushner's *When Children Ask About God* (New York: Schocken, 1989) is, like all of Rabbi Kushner's writing, both accessible and wise. Rabbi Marc Gellman and Monsignor Thomas Hartman collaborated on a book that can be read together with your children, called *Where Does God Live?* (New York: Ballantine Books, 1992). An excellent book for Jewish parents and children to read is *God and the Story of Judaism* by Dorothy K. Kripke and Meyer Levin (New York: Behrman, 1962). Dorothy Kripke also wrote a book for young children called *Let's Talk About God* (New York: Behrman House, 1953). Also helpful is Jean Grasso Fitzpatrick's *Something More: Nurturing Your Child's Spiritual Growth* (New York: Viking Penguin, 1992), which has an extensive bibliography of music and books from various traditions.

For parents seeking insight into the spirituality of chil
dren, David Heller's *The Children's God* (Chicago: University of Chicago Press, 1988), based on numerous interviews
with children of different faiths, is an interesting work. A
classic in the field is Robert Coles's *The Spiritual Life of Children* (Boston: Houghton Mifflin, 1990), part of Coles's series
of books on the inner life of children.

Worshipping Together with Questioning Minds by Sylvia
Lyon Fahs (Boston: Beacon Press, 1965) is illuminating, particularly on the subject of children and prayer. The different
developmental stages of belief have been analyzed in James
Fowler's widely acclaimed *Stages of Faith* (San Francisco:
Harper and Row, 1981), which is based on the work of
theorists like Kohlberg, Erickson, and Piaget.

For Jewish legal sources on children, *The Jewish Child:
Halakhic Perspectives* by Shoshana Matzner-Bekerman (New
York: K'tav, 1984) is a handy compendium.

The question of talking to children about death is sensi-
tively handled in an anthology culled from several disciplines
and faith traditions, *Explaining Death to Children* (Boston:
Beacon Press, 1969), Earl Grollman, ed. *New Meanings of
Death* (New York: McGraw-Hill, 1977), edited by Herman
Feifel, also has helpful material. Elisabeth Kübler-Ross,
who has done important work in the field of bereavement
and death, has written on children as well in *On Children
and Death* (New York: Macmillan, 1985). And *The Kids'
Book About Death and Dying: By and for kids* (Boston: Little
Brown and Co., 1985), edited by Eric E. Rofes and the
Fayerweather Street School staff, is a book you can
read along with your children as they struggle to handle
death.

There Is a Rainbow Behind Every Dark Cloud (edited by the Center for Attitudinal Healing staff) was written by children with life-threatening illnesses (New York: Celestial Arts, 1979) and makes for poignant reading. Jill Krementz's *How It Feels When a Parent Dies* (New York: Alfred Knopf, 1988) also uses children's own words to express what this devastating loss means to a child.

For an insight into how a child's mind works, there are the charming collections by Eric Marshall and Stuart Hample, *Children's Letters to God* (New York: Fontana, 1975) and *Children's Letters to God: The New Collection*, illustrated by Tom Bloom (New York: Workman Pub., 1991). Selma Fraiberg's *Magic Years* (New York: Macmillan, 1981), although not specifically about religion, is a wonderful peek into the mental world of a child.

For parents who would like guidance in how to set up a Jewish home, a lot of help is available. Some of the best work being done in family education is at the Whizin Center of the University of Judaism under the direction of Dr. Ron Wolfson. Dr. Wolfson has produced several books in the "Art of Jewish Living" series (New York: Federation of Jewish Men's Clubs): *A Time to Mourn . . . A Time to Comfort* (1993); *The Passover Seder* (1988); *Hanukkah* (1990); *The Shabbat Seder* (1985).

Hayim Halevy Donin's *To Raise a Jewish Child* (New York: Basic Books, 1991) takes the reader through a traditional cycle of Jewish life up to marriage. It also has a helpful list of resources. Also from an Orthodox perspective is Blu Greenberg's *How to Run a Traditional Jewish Household* (New York: Aronson, 1989). From a Reform perspective, Daniel B. Syme's *The Jewish Home: A Guide for Jewish Living*

(Northvale, NJ: Aronson, 1992) uses an easily understood question-and-answer format.

Parents interested in Jewish song might try *Books of Hasidic Music* (two volumes) by Velvel Pasternak (New York: Bloch Pub. Co., 1971); *Children's Songs* by Emanuel Barkan (New York: Jewish Education Press, 1976); and *Israel in Song* by Velvel Pasternak (New York: Jewish Education Press, 1974). Many more books, as well as tapes and CDs, are available. Check your local book or music store.

The Harvard Hillel Sabbath Songbook by Ben-Zion Gold contains words and music in Hebrew, English, and Yiddish to scores of standard Sabbath songs as well as some modern Israeli songs. The songbook also contains Sabbath blessings (Boston: David R. Godine, 1992).

Index

demands of, 13–14, 39, 68, 73,
79–80, 84
non-Jewish, 76, 114, 115–16,
128–33, 143, 215
pagan, 69, 210
politics in, 218–19
purposes of, 11, 14, 31
search and struggle in, 8–10
tolerance and, 114, 128–33,
224
see also faith
religious education:
adult study and, 8, 10–13
daily life and example in, 25–
26, 216–17
inadequacies of, 8–9
inadvertent messages in, 25–26,
47–49
keeping issues alive in, 25–26
purposes of, 73, 109
struggle and development in,
8–10
teachers of, xiii, 8–9, 25–26,
101, 217–18, 220–21
repentance, 136–40, 210
three steps to, 137–38
resistance fighters, 176
Ribon Haolam, 148
ritual:
communication through, 99–
102
experiment and practice with,
20–22, 104–5
family, 18, 20–22, 30–31, 46,
99–105, 226
gesture and symbolism of, 101
grief, 86, 155, 196, 200–201,
212
humor in, 30–31, 100
individual customs and, 20–21,
22
non-Jewish, 131

nonobservance of, 102, 104,
129
place of children in, 29–32
purposes of, 18–19, 100–102,
103
Sabbath, 18, 20–22, 94, 99–
101, 104, 123–25, 163, 226,
229
sanctity and, 18–21, 99–105
secular, 18, 24
self-consciousness of, 20, 21,
101
self-understanding and, 19
significance and power of, 18–
22, 99–105
rivalry, 106, 121, 134
Rocky Mountains, 89–90
Rothblum, Moshe, 47–48
Russell, Bertrand, 10
Ruth, 80, 81

Sabbath, 161–63
meals of, 20–22, 99–101
resting on, 161–62
rituals of, 18, 20–22, 94, 99–
101, 104, 123–25, 163, 226,
229
services on, 47–48
singing and, 163
Sabbath, The (Heschel), 161
sacredness:
joy and, 21, 33
moments of, 1, 5–6, 14–15,
18–21, 53, 54, 86, 89–90,
97, 99–105
ritual and, 18–21, 99–105
in sanctuaries, 2, 3, 6, 163
sacrifices, 107, 210
burning of, 69
Salanter, Yisroel, 139
Salovey, Peter, 182
Samuel, 67, 93

wine, 20, 30, 101, 226
wizardry, 43
wonder, 19
  cultivating a sense of, 13, 33–
    34, 36, 41–43
  faith and, 13, 41
  substituting certainty for, 12
working, 148, 162
world:
  adult views of, 47
  appreciation of, 29, 33, 40, 41–
    43, 45, 53, 89–90
  beauty of, 13–14, 54, 64, 86,
    89–90, 111, 130, 204
  children's views of, 47–51,
    53
  creation of, 34, 42, 45, 54, 58,
    72, 73, 87, 117, 122, 140,
    161–62, 174, 204

essential goodness of, 7, 11,
  117, 118
God's presence in, 86–92
interdependence in, 140–42
knowledge of, 26, 29, 67, 68
redemption of, 30–32, 90, 122,
  215
repairing of, 140–42, 225
worry, 39, 98
Writings, 72n

Yale University, 182
yetzer hara, 120
yetzer hatov, 120
Yom Kippur, 122, 137

zealotry, 225–26
Zohar, 160
Zusya, Rabbi, 224–25